Star Log Cabin

Q ★ U ★ I ★ L ★ T

from the Quilt in a Day® Series   *by Eleanor Burns*

For Orion...

...a Star

Published by Quilt in a Day®, Inc.

1955 Diamond Street, San Marcos, CA 92069

Copyright 1995 Eleanor A. Burns Family Trust

First Printing, March, 1995

ISBN 0-922705-86-0

Art Direction, Merritt Voigtlander

Photography, Wayne Norton

TABLE OF CONTENTS

PRAIRIE PIONEER QUILTERS
of GRAND ISLAND, NEBRASKA

Fabric Selection

Begin with one multicolored print. From that one print, select three **contrasting** color families for A, B and Star.

A B Star

It might help you to think of the quilt as...

- light, medium, and dark,
- medium, medium, and dark,
- or medium, dark, and dark.

Vary the scales of the prints for interest, as small, medium, large, and one that reads solid.

Select 100% cotton fabrics, at least 42" wide. Paste up fabric swatches on page 7.

Parts of the Block

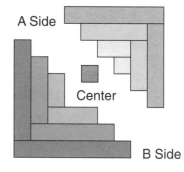

A Side

Center

B Side

A Side needs four different fabrics, A❶❷❸❹, usually from the same color family. Select fabrics with a slight gradation in the color, or with all the same value.

B Side also needs four different fabrics, B❶❷❸❹, either with gradation or similar values.

The Center ● of the block is generally a solid fabric or one that reads solid from a distance. Pull it from the multicolor print to tie the A and B color families together.

Parts Surrounding the Block

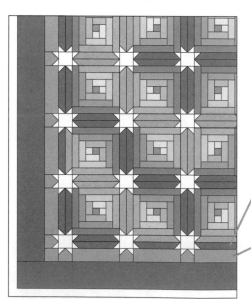

The Star ○ should be a great color contrast or value contrast to the block, particularly with fabrics A❹ and B❹. The Center of the block and the Star can be the same fabric.

The Frame ●, a narrow border surrounding the blocks, can be any fabric except A❹, B❹, or Star fabric and should read solid from a distance.

The First or Only Border ● can be any fabric but Star or Frame.

Parts of the Quilt

Log Cabin Blocks
A ❶ ❷ ❸
CENTER ●
B ❶ ❷ ❸

are fast and easy to make from 2" wide strips. The specified seam allowance is ¼". Once the blocks are constructed, the remaining measurements are based on your personal seam and pressing technique.

The Lattice
A❹ and/or B❹

is cut ⅛" larger than your average block size to compensate for "shrinkage" from the Star Points.

The Frame
A❹ or B❹
FRAME ●

is also cut ⅛" larger than your average block size.

The 1st Border
1st BORDER ●

is cut the same size as the Block.

Size of your Block

Block

Lattice
Block plus ⅛"

Frame
Block plus ⅛"

Border
Size of Block

These three pieces are identical in width...

the width of the Lattice,

the width of the Star Centers,

and the width of the Border.

Width of your Lattice

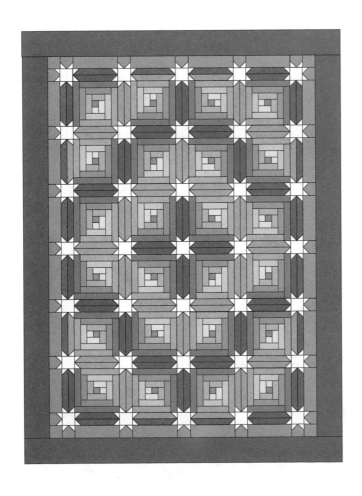

Supplies

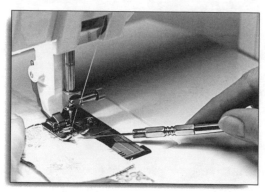

- Stiletto

- Large rotary cutter with new blade

Plexiglass rulers

- 6" x 24" long ruler
- 6" x 12" ruler
- 6" square ruler
- 12 ½" Square Up ruler

- Gridded cutting mat
- Gridded pressing mat

For machine quilting

- Invisible thread
- Quilt clips
- Binder clips or masking tape
- Walking foot attachment
- Pinning tool
- 1" Safety pins

Paste-Up Sheet

Approximate block size 13½"

Label your fabric as it is "cut" at the fabric store.
Paste up fabric swatches.

Center   Star

A1   A2   A3   Set aside
                  until blocks—
                  are sewn.   A4

B1   B2   B3   B4

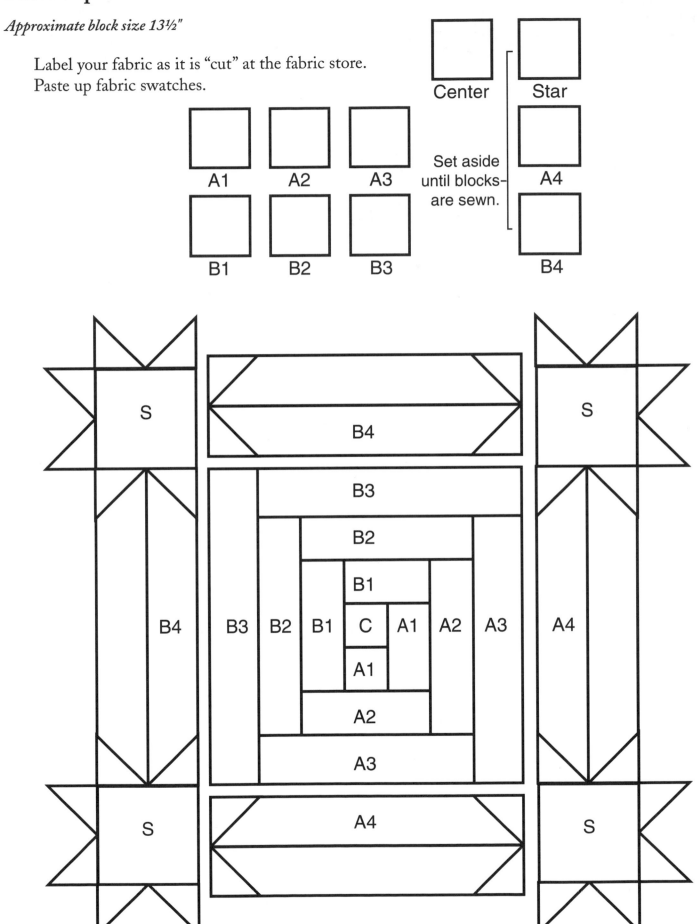

Yardage & Cutting Charts

Wallhanging

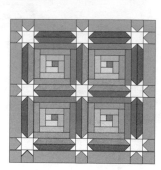

4 Blocks
Approximate finished size: 35" x 35"
Choose 100% cotton fabric,
at least 42" wide.

Blocks				cut strips selvage to selvage
Center	⬤	⅛ yd	1	2" wide strip
Fabric A ❶		⅛ yd	1	2" wide strip
Fabric A ❷		¼ yd	2	2" wide strips
Fabric A ❸		¼ yd	2	2" wide strips
Fabric A ❹		⅓ yd	4	2" wide strips
Fabric B ❶		⅛ yd	1	2" wide strip
Fabric B ❷		¼ yd	2	2" wide strips
Fabric B ❸		¼ yd	3	2" wide strips
Fabric B ❹		⅓ yd	4	2" wide strips

Star *may be same fabric as Center*			
Star	◯	½ yd	cut after blocks are sewn and measured

Frame *any fabric but Star, Fabric A❹ or B❹*				
Frame	⬤	⅓ yd	4	2" wide strips

Border *any fabric but Star or Frame*			
Only	⬤	½ yd	cut later

Finish				
Batting	☐	40"	square	
Backing	⬤	1⅛ yds		
Binding	⬤	½ yd	4	3" wide strips

LAP ROBE

12 Blocks
Approximate finished size: 48" x 62"
Choose 100% cotton fabric,
at least 42" wide.

Blocks				*cut strips selvage to selvage*
Center	●	⅛ yd	1	*2" wide strip*
Fabric A	①	¼ yd	3	*2" wide strips*
Fabric A	②	⅓ yd	4	*2" wide strips*
Fabric A	③	½ yd	6	*2" wide strips*
Fabric A	④	⅝ yd	8	*2" wide strips*
Fabric B	❶	⅓ yd	3	*2" wide strips*
Fabric B	❷	½ yd	5	*2" wide strips*
Fabric B	❸	⅝ yd	8	*2" wide strips*
Fabric B	❹	⅝ yd	8	*2" wide strips*

Star *may be same fabric as Center*				
Star	○	1 yd		*cut after blocks are sewn and measured*

Frame *any fabric but Star, Fabric A④ or B④*				
Frame	●	½ yd	6	*2" wide strips*

Border *any fabric but Star or Frame*				
Only	●	⅔ yd		*cut later*

Finish				
Batting	☐	55" x 70"		
Backing	●	4 yds	2	*equal pieces*
Binding	●	¾ yd	6	*3" wide strips*

9

Twin

Blocks | | | | cut strips selvage to selvage

Blocks				*cut strips selvage to selvage*
Center	●	⅛ yd	1	2" wide strip
Fabric A ❶		¼ yd	3	2" wide strips
Fabric A ❷		⅜ yd	5	2" wide strips
Fabric A ❸		½ yd	7	2" wide strips
Fabric A ❹		⅔ yd	10	2" wide strips
Fabric B ❶		⅓ yd	4	2" wide strips
Fabric B ❷		½ yd	6	2" wide strips
Fabric B ❸		⅔ yd	10	2" wide strips
Fabric B ❹		⅔ yd	10	2" wide strips

Star *may be same fabric as Center*

Star	○	1 yd		*cut after blocks are sewn and measured*

Frame *any fabric but Star, Fabric A❹ or B❹*

Frame	●	½ yd	6	2" wide strips

Border *any fabric but Star or Frame*

1st	●	¾ yd		*cut later*
Narrow Border (optional)	●	½ yd	7	2" wide strips
2nd	●	1½ yds	8	5½" wide strips
3rd	●	2 yds	9	7½" wide strips

Finish

Batting	☐	90" x 108"		
Backing	●	6 yds	2	equal pieces
Binding	●	⅞ yd	9	3" wide strips

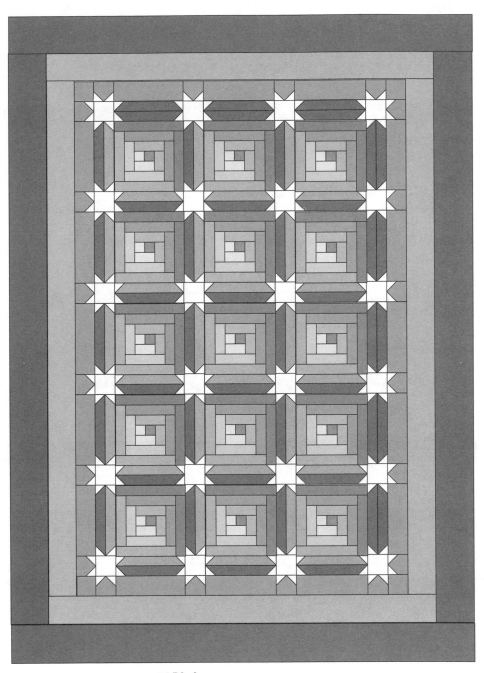

15 Blocks
Approximate finished size: 70" x 96"
Choose 100% cotton fabric,
at least 42" wide.

Double /Queen Coverlet

Blocks				cut strips selvage to selvage
Center	●	¼ yd	2	2" wide strips
Fabric A ❶		⅓ yd	4	2" wide strips
Fabric A ❷		½ yd	7	2" wide strips
Fabric A ❸		¾ yd	11	2" wide strips
Fabric A ❹		1⅛ yds	17	2" wide strips
Fabric B ❶		½ yd	6	2" wide strips
Fabric B ❷		⅝ yd	9	2" wide strips
Fabric B ❸		1 yd	16	2" wide strips
Fabric B ❹		1⅛ yds	17	2" wide strips

Star *may be same fabric as Center*				
Star	○	1⅓ yds		cut after blocks are sewn and measured

Frame *any fabric but Star, Fabric A❹ or B❹*				
Frame	●	½ yd	7	2" wide strips

Border *any fabric but Star or Frame*				
1st	●	1 yd	cut later	
Narrow Border (optional)	●	⅝ yd	8	2" wide strips
2nd	●	1⅓ yds	9	4½" wide strips
3rd	●	2 yds	10	6½" wide strips

Finish				
Batting	☐	120"	square	
Backing (Measure top & fabric width)	●	6¾ yds	2	equal pieces or
		10 yds	3	equal pieces
Binding	●	1⅛ yds	11	3" wide strips

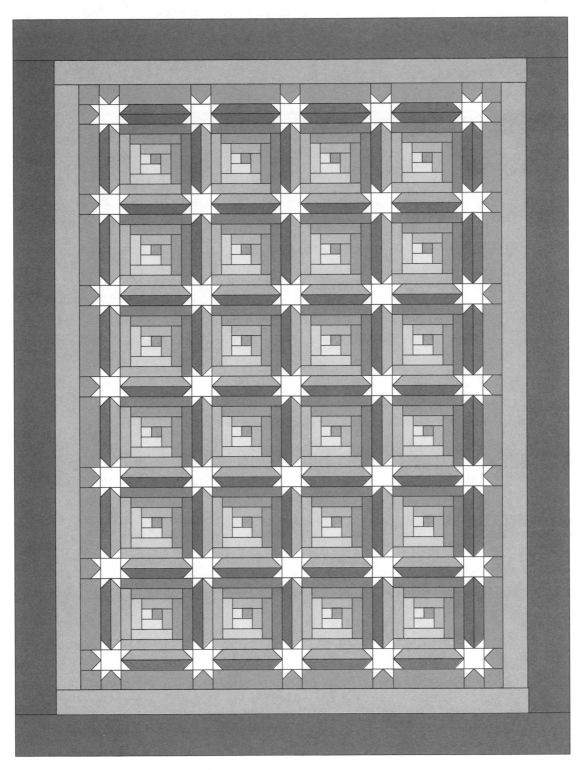

24 Blocks
Approximate finished size: 82" x 108"
Choose 100% cotton fabric,
at least 42" wide.

Queen Bedspread/King

Blocks				*cut strips selvage to selvage*
Center	●	¼ yd	2	2" wide strips
Fabric A	❶	⅜ yd	5	2" wide strips
Fabric A	❷	⅔ yd	11	2" wide strips
Fabric A	❸	1⅛ yds	17	2" wide strips
Fabric A	❹	1½ yds	24	2" wide strips
Fabric B	❶	⅝ yd	8	2" wide strips
Fabric B	❷	1 yd	14	2" wide strips
Fabric B	❸	1¼ yds	21	2" wide strips
Fabric B	❹	1½ yds	24	2" wide strips

Star *may be same fabric as Center*			
Star	○	1⅞ yds	*cut after blocks are sewn and measured*

Frame *any fabric but Star, Fabric A❹ or B❹*				
Frame	●	⅝ yd	8	2" wide strips

Border *any fabric but Star or Frame*				
1st	●	1⅛ yds	*cut later*	
Narrow Border (optional)	●	⅔ yd	10	2" wide strips
2nd	●	1⅔ yds	10	5½" wide strips
3rd	●	2½ yds	11	7½" wide strips

Finish				
Batting	☐	120"	*square*	
Backing	●	10 yds	3	*equal pieces*
Binding	●	1⅛ yds	11	3" wide strips

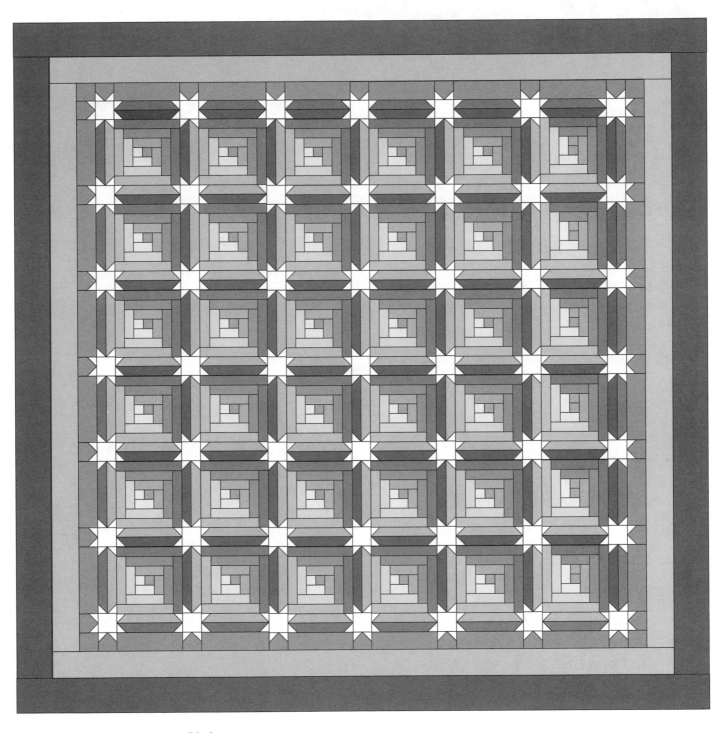

36 Blocks
Approximate finished size: 112" x 112"
Choose 100% cotton fabric,
at least 42" wide.

Cutting Strips

Use a large rotary cutter with a sharp blade and a 6" x 24" plexiglass ruler on a gridded cutting mat. Check that the measurements are the same on the ruler and the gridded cutting mat.

1. Make a nick on the selvage edge, and tear your fabric from selvage to selvage to put the fabric on the straight of the grain.

2. Fold the fabric in half, matching the torn straight edge thread to thread.

3. With the fold of the fabric at the top, line up the torn edge of fabric on the gridded cutting mat with the left edge extended slightly to the left of zero. Reverse this procedure if you are left-handed.

4. Line up the 6" x 24" ruler on zero. Spread the fingers of your left hand to hold the ruler firmly. With the rotary cutter in your right hand, begin cutting with the blade off the fabric on the mat. Put all your strength into the rotary cutter as you cut away from you, and trim the torn, ragged edge.

5. Accuracy is important. For blocks: Lift, and move the ruler until it lines up with the 2" strip width on the grid and cut. For Borders: Fabrics are cut at different widths. Refer to your Yardage Chart.

6. Open the first strip to see if it is straight. Check periodically. Make a straightening tear when necessary.

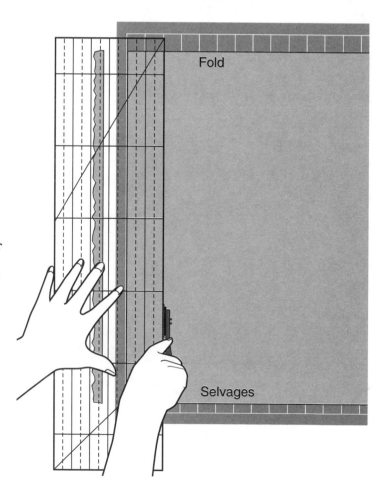

Fold

Selvages

Sewing and Pressing

Stitch Length

Use a small stitch, 12 to 15 to the inch, or a setting of #2.

¼" Seam Allowance

Use a consistent seam allowance through-out the construction of the quilt. If necessary, adjust the needle position, change the presser foot, or feed the fabric under the presser foot to achieve the ¼".

Serging

A person experienced with serging can construct the blocks and sew the top together with a serger. A five thread serger is recommended. Carefully match seam allowances when changing machines.

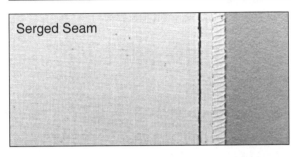
Regular Seam

Serged Seam

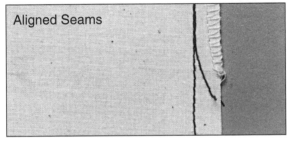

Aligned Seams

Optional Pressing

It's not necessary to press log cabin blocks after each step of construction as long as you pull and fingerpress seams flat before stitching over them.

However, if you prefer to press during construction, press after cutting the blocks apart.

1. Turn stack over.

2. Press to set the seam.

3. Lift up top strip and press flat.

   Always press seam away from center square.

Refer to the strip sewing illustrations for block placement.

Arranging the Strips

1. Place the 2" strips to the right of your sewing machine in sewing order.

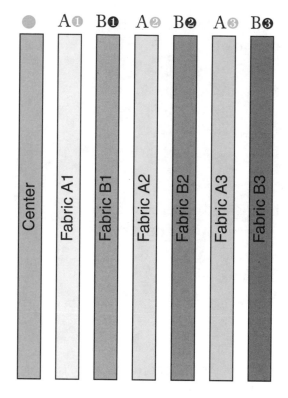

2. Set aside strips A❹ and B❹ until needed for "Lattice."

set aside

Making the Center Squares

1. Place a Center strip right sides together to an A❶ strip.

2. Sew the two strips together lengthwise, with Center on the top.

    Use a ¼" seam allowance and 15 stitches per inch, or a #2 stitch setting.

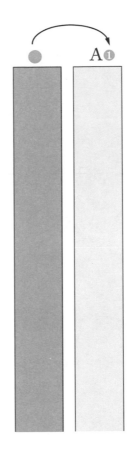

If you have a second Center strip, sew a second set.

Sew this many strips	
Wallhanging	¼ strip
Lap Robe	¾ strip
Twin	1 strip
Double-Queen	1¼ strips
Queen-King	2 strips

3. Lay sewn strips on a cutting mat. Square off the left end, removing the selvages.

4. Cut into 2" squares using the 6" x 6" ruler and rotary cutter.

5. Stack.

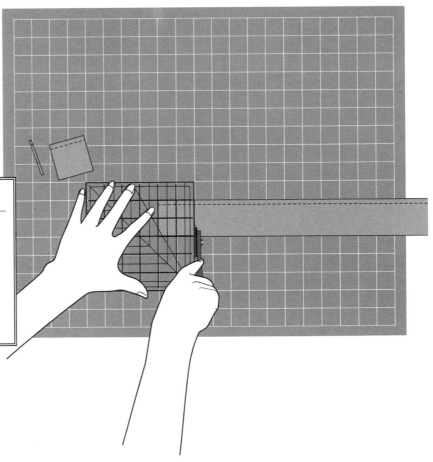

Cut this many Center squares	
Wallhanging	4
Lap Robe	12
Twin	15
Double-Queen	24
Queen-King	36

6. Center fabric is used only once in the block. Remove Center left-overs from area.
    All other fabrics are used twice in each block.

Adding another Fabric A❶ Strip

For optional pressing see page 17.

1. Turn stack over so A❶ is on top.

2. Place an A❶ strip right side up under the presser foot and stitch an inch to hold the strip in place.

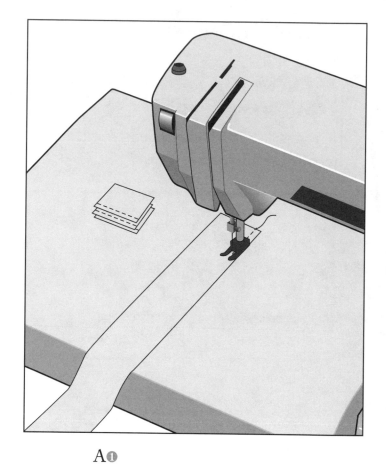

A❶

3. Open and place a block right sides together to the strip with A❶ at the top.

4. Anchor with an inch of stitching.

5. Sew, fingerpressing the seam allowance up toward A❶. Use the stiletto to hold the seam flat.

6. As you near the end of the block, pick up the second block and unfold it.

7. Butt it after the first block.

8. Sew all blocks, always placing A❶ toward the top, and pressing the seam allowance up.

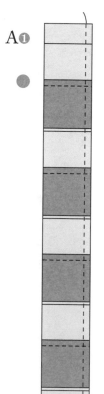

A❶

Stop and pull block so there are no puckers or tucks at the seam.

Fingerpress seam up.

9. When there is not enough strip for an additional block, start a new strip.

10. Lay strips on cutting mat along a grid line.

11. Line up a 6" x 6" ruler with the outside edge, and cut between blocks. Trim if necessary.

12. Stack.

13. A❶ has been used twice in the block. Remove any extra A❶ strips from the sewing area.

Trim between blocks if necessary. Cut straight edges.

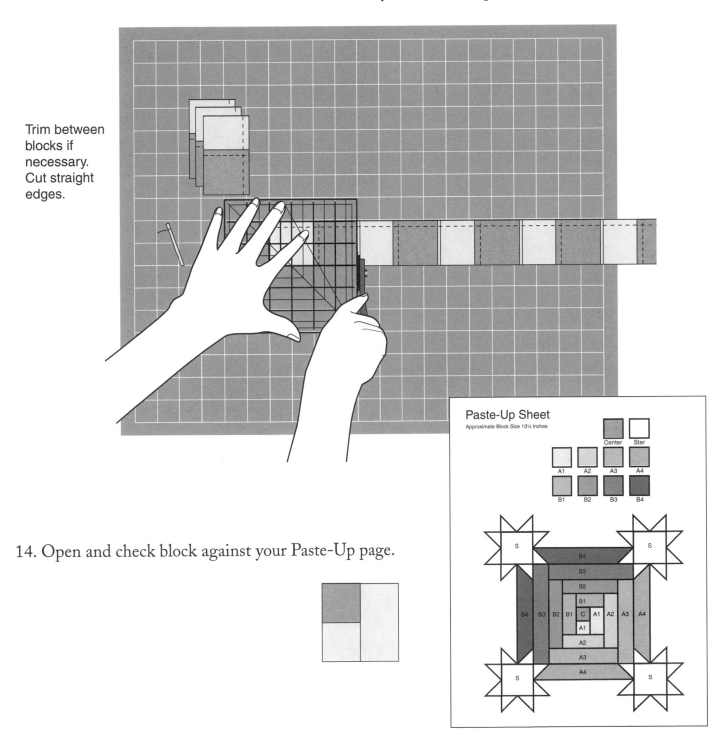

14. Open and check block against your Paste-Up page.

Paste-Up Sheet
Approximate Block Size 13½ Inches

21

Adding the First B❶ Strip

1. Turn stack over so A❶ strip just added is on the top. Line up the block so the stitching is parallel with the table.

2. Place a B❶ strip under presser foot, right side up.

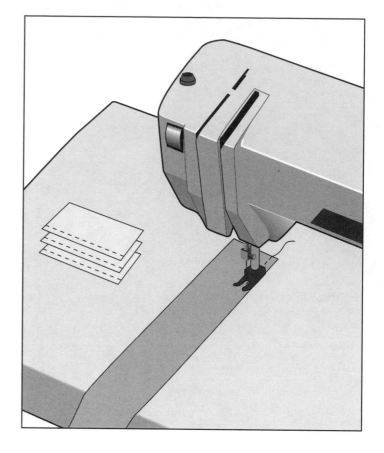

3. Open and place block right sides together to strip, with A❶ strip across the top.

4. Sew the length of the block, fingerpressing the seam up and flat. The stiletto is also useful for directing seams.

5. Continue butting on next blocks, until a B❶ strip has been added to all blocks. Remember to anticipate the ends and start a new strip as needed.

6. Lay strip on cutting mat, with blocks on top.

7. Cut apart between blocks. Stack.

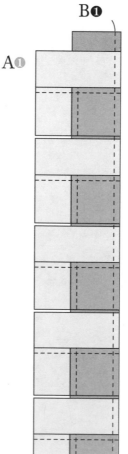

B❶

A❶

Stop and pull block so there are no puckers or tucks at the seam.

Fingerpress seam up.

Fingerpress seam up.

Adding the Second B❶ Strip

1. Turn stack over so B❶ is on top. Line up the stack so the stitching is parallel with the table.

   Think of the strip on the top, B❶, as the "handle." The handle is always placed at the top of the next strip.

2. Place a B❶ strip under presser foot, right side up.

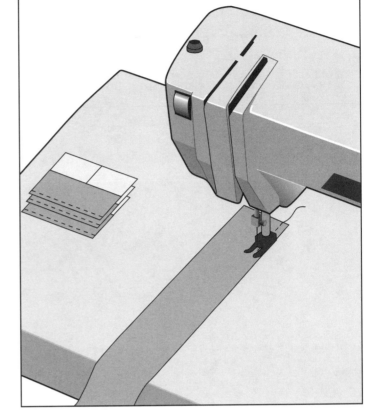

3. Open and place block with first B❶ strip across top and perpendicular to second B❶ strip.

4. Sew the length of the block, pushing the first seam up and flat, and the second seam down and flat.

   As the block construction progresses, there will be these two seams. Always push the first seam up and flat, and second seam down and flat.

5. Continue butting and sewing blocks, and adding new strips as necessary until the second B❶ strip is added to all blocks.

6. Cut apart between blocks. Stack.

7. B❶ strips have been added twice to each block. Remove extra B❶ strips from sewing area.

8. Check block against your Paste-Up page.

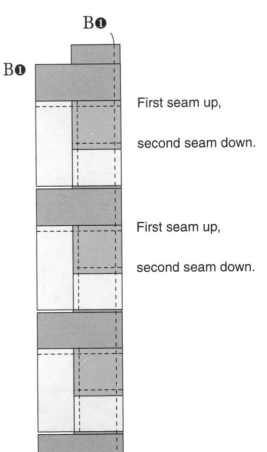

B❶

B❶

First seam up,

second seam down.

First seam up,

second seam down.

Adding the A❷ Strips

1. Turn stack over. Line up the stack so the stitching and "handle" are parallel with the table.

2. Place an A❷ strip under presser foot, right side up.

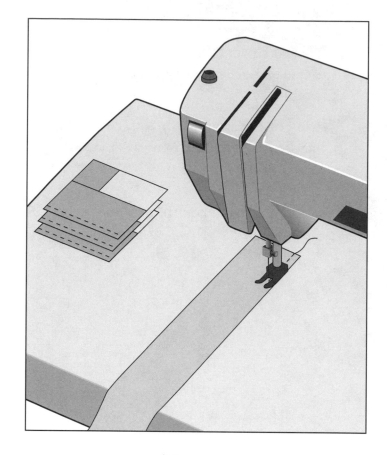

3. Open and place block with second B❶ strip across top and perpendicular to the new strip.

4. Sew all blocks, pushing first seams up and second seams down. The wrong side of the block lies flat from the Center out.

5. Cut apart. Stack.

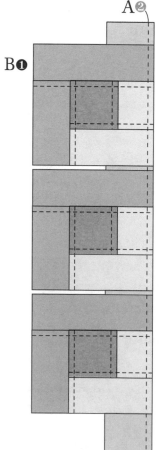

A❷

B❶

Seams lie flat from the center out.

6. Turn stack over. Line up stitching and "handle" parallel with table.

7. Place a second A❷ strip under presser foot.

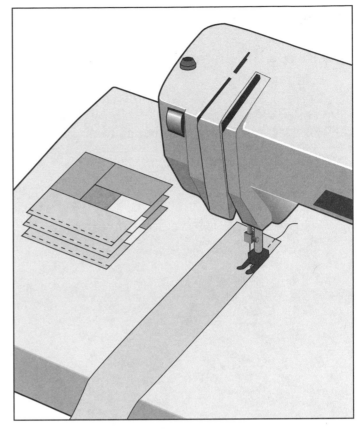

8. Open and place block with first A❷ strip, the "handle," across top and perpendicular to new strip.

9. Sew all blocks.

10. Cut apart. Stack.

11. Turn stack over. Line up stitching and "handle" parallel with table.

12. A❷ strips have been added twice to each block. Remove extra A❷ strips from sewing area.

A❷

A❷

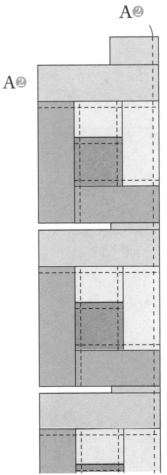

Adding B❷ Strips

1. Place a B❷ strip under presser foot, right side up.

2. Open and place block with second A❷ strip across top and perpendicular to new strip.

3. Sew all blocks.

4. Cut apart. Stack.

5. Turn stack over. Line up stitching and "handle" parallel with table.

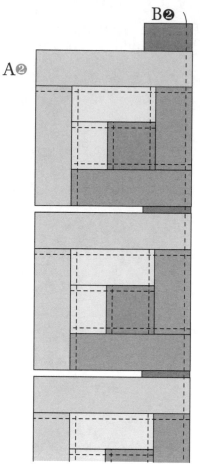

6. Place a second B❷ strip under presser foot.

7. Open and place block with B❷ across top.

8. Sew all blocks.

9. Cut apart. Stack.

10. Turn stack over. Line up stitching and "handle" parallel with table.

11. Remove extra B❷ strips from sewing area.

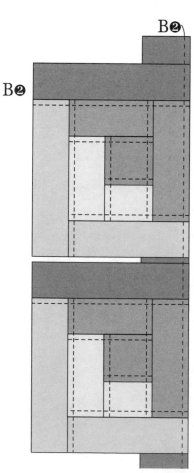

Adding A③ Strips

1. Place an A③ strip under presser foot.

2. Open and place block with B② across top.

3. Sew all blocks.

4. Cut apart. Stack.

5. Turn stack over. Line up stitching and "handle" parallel with table.

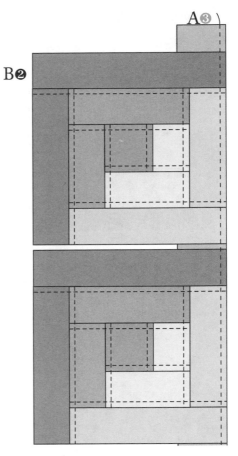

6. Place a second A③ strip under presser foot.

7. Open and place block with A③ across top.

8. Sew all blocks.

9. Cut apart. Stack.

10. Turn stack over. Line up stitching and "handle" parallel with table.

11. Remove extra A③ strips from sewing area.

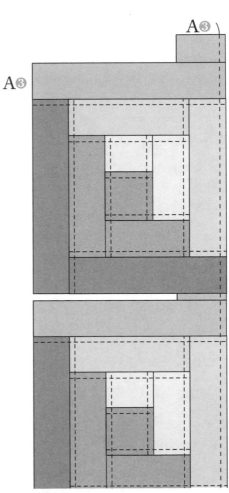

Adding B❸ Strips

1. Place a B❸ strip under presser foot.

2. Open and place block with A❸ across top.

3. Sew all blocks.

4. Cut apart. Stack.

5. Turn stack over. Line up stitching and "handle" parallel with table.

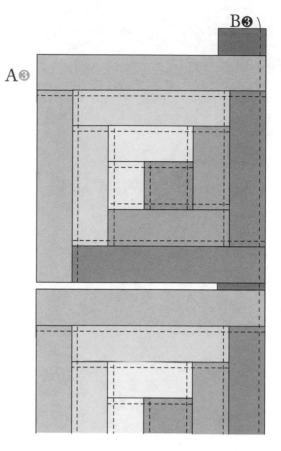

6. Place a second B❸ strip under presser foot.

7. Open and place block with B❸ across top.

8. Sew all blocks.

9. Cut apart. Stack.

10. Turn stack over.

11. Remove extra B❸ strips from sewing area.

Do not add A❹ and B❹ to the blocks.

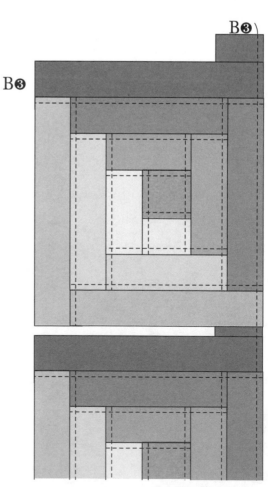

Pressing the Block

1. Press each block from the right side.

2. Press from the wrong side, making sure there are no tucks at the seams.

3. Measure several to find an average size, 10½" to 11", depending on your seam allowance.

4. Re-press blocks that are smaller than your determined average size.

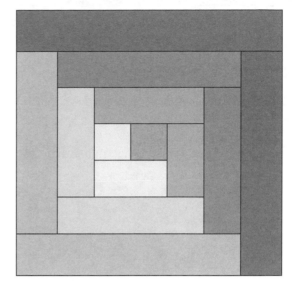

10½" to 11"
average size.

5. Sliver trim larger blocks equally on four sides to your average size.

 • Place the diagonal line of the 12½" ruler across the center of the block.

 • Trim on two sides.

 • Turn, and trim equal amounts on the remaining two sides.

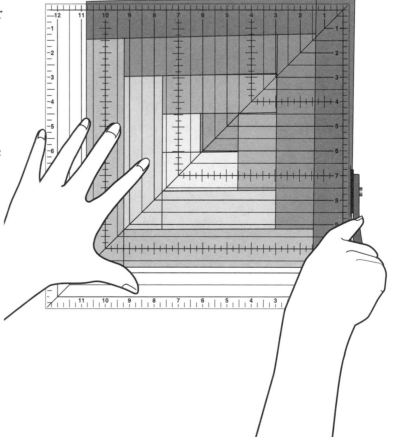

Record your
Average Block Size

approximately 10½" - 11"

6. Transfer this measurement to page 5.

1. Study the various layouts for your size quilt. The dark shading within the block represents the shading of Side B.

    Mark your layout page with a paper clip or Post-it™ note.

2. Lay out your blocks to find your favorite, following the shading in each. Allow space between the blocks for the "Lattice" that will soon be added.

3. Place A❹ strips beside A❸, and B❹ strips beside B❸ to help see the pattern.

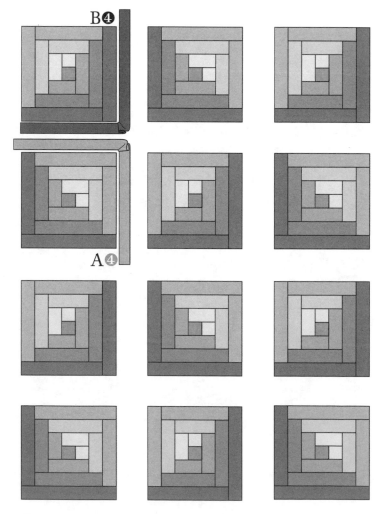

Example of a Lap Robe, Mountains layout.

4. Referring to your selected layout, note the fabrics and number needed for Lattice.

Fabric A ④
Fabric A ④

Sew at least 1 strip of each together. Cut them into 4 pieces.

Fabric B ④
Fabric B ④

Sew at least 1 strip of each together. Cut them into 4 pieces.

Fabric A ④
Fabric B ④

Sew at least 3 strips of each together. Cut them into 9 pieces.

Example of a Lap Robe, Mountains layout.

5. Stack the 2" x 42" strips of A④ and B④ in equal piles according to your choice. Your layout may not require all three of these.

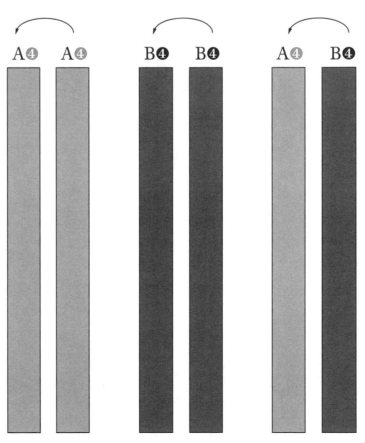

A④ A④   B④ B④   A④ B④

6. Assembly-line sew them together lengthwise in pairs.

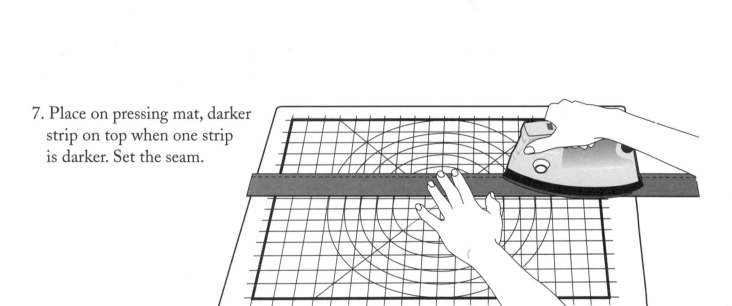

7. Place on pressing mat, darker
   strip on top when one strip
   is darker. Set the seam.

8. Lift strip and press seam
   allowance toward the
   top strip.

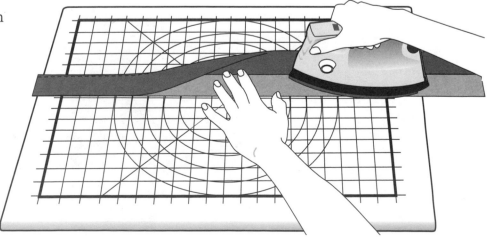

9. Referring to page 5, record the average size of your block.

   Add ⅛" to compensate for shrinkage after sewing on Star Points. This measurement is the size to cut your Lattice.

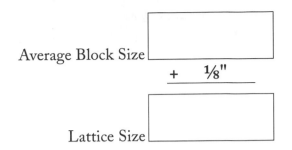

Average Block Size ☐

+   ⅛"

Lattice Size ☐

10. Layer cut the required number of Lattice from each pair of strips according to your choice.

   You will get 3 or 4 Lattice from each paired strip. If you get only 3, you need to sew more strips together to get the required number. The Yardage and Cutting Chart allowed for these extra strips.

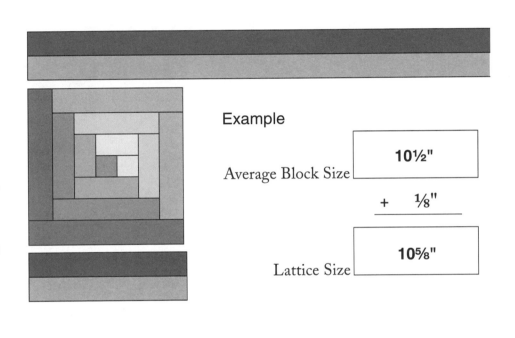

Example

Average Block Size | **10½"**

+   ⅛"

Lattice Size | **10⅝"**

11. Stack and set aside until 2" squares for Star Points are marked and cut.

Cutting the Star Centers from Star Fabric

1. Measure several Lattice to find the average width.

Record your average width

approximately 3½"

2. Transfer this measurement to page 5.

Approximately 3½"

3. Cut strips your measurement selvage to selvage from the Star fabric for the Star Centers.

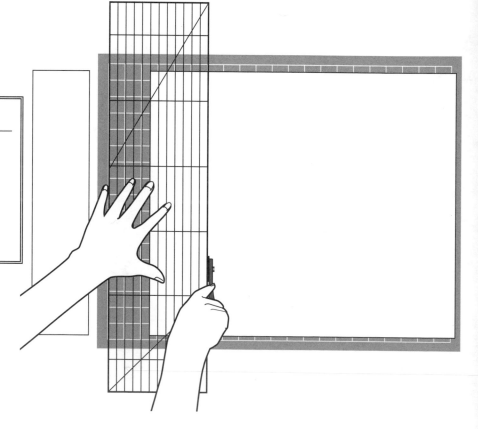

Cut this many strips

Wallhanging	 1
Lap Robe	 2
Twin	 2
Double-Queen	 3
Queen-King	 5

4. From those strips, cut the required number of Star Center Squares.

Cut this many Star Centers	
Wallhanging	.9
Lap Robe	.20
Twin	.24
Double-Queen	.35
Queen-King	.49

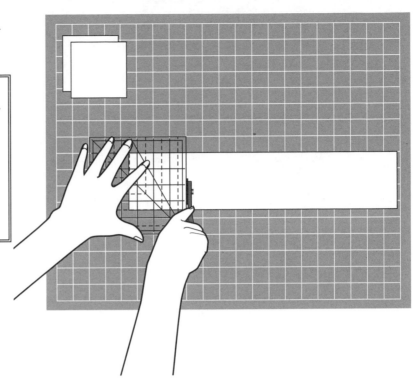

Cutting 11" Strips for Star Points

Cut Star fabric into 11" wide strips selvage to selvage according to your quilt size.

Cut this many strips	
Wallhanging	.1
Lap Robe	.2
Twin	.2
Double-Queen	.3
Queen-King	.4

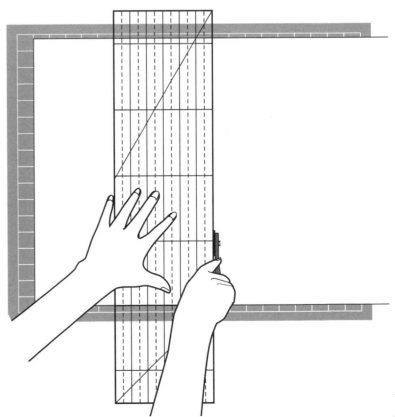

35

Marking 2" Squares with Diagonal Lines

Star Points are made by sewing on diagonal lines drawn on 2" squares of Star fabric.

Select one of these techniques for marking 2" squares with diagonal lines onto the fabric.

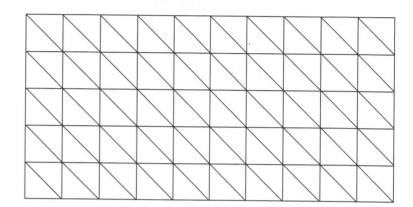

- transferring lines with an iron-on sheet
- drawing lines on fabric with pencil (see next page.)

The easiest method is transferring lines with an iron-on sheet. Pre-printed heat transfer sheets of the 2" grid are provided at the back of this book. Instructions for heat transfer are also on these pages.

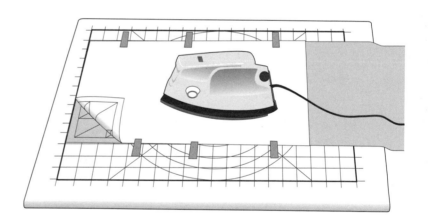

If the heat transferred ink does not show up on the wrong side of your star fabric, trace the grid with a heat transfer pen in a suitable color.

If the lines from the heat transfer do not show on your fabric, you may also draw the lines with a pencil.

Drawing 2" Grid Lines on Fabric

1. Cut each strip in half on the fold to make two manageable 11" pieces.

2. Place **wrong side up** on gridded cutting mat.

3. Place ½" excess fabric to left of zero.

4. **Draw** on 2" vertical lines with a sharp pencil. Back off the ruler a pencil line width so lines fall exactly in 2" increments. Lines must be accurate.

   Use a light pencil on dark fabrics, and a dark pencil on light fabrics.

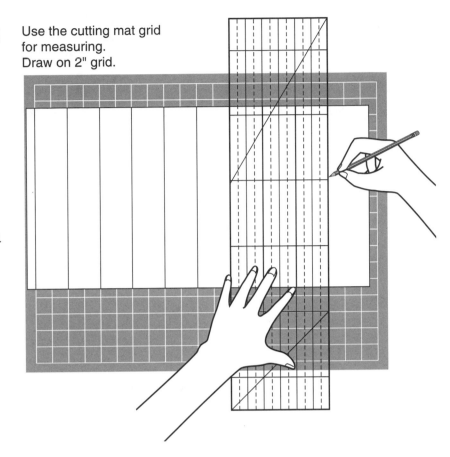

Use the cutting mat grid for measuring. Draw on 2" grid.

5. **Draw** on 2" horizontal lines. Allow ½" excess fabric on outside edges.

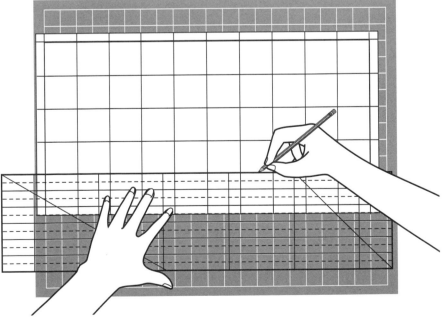

Allow an extra ½" on all four sides.

6. Carefully draw diagonal lines through squares. Back off the ruler a pencil line width, so the line falls exactly corner to corner.

The lines must be drawn corner to corner on each square.

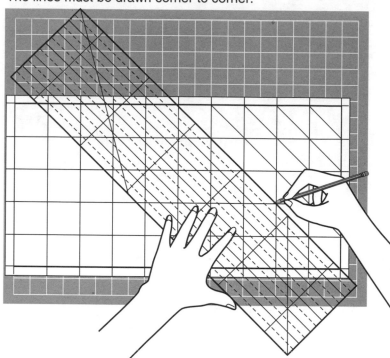

7. Cut on the square lines only.

You need this many squares	
Wallhanging 72	
Lap Robe 160	
Twin 192	
Double-Queen 280	
Queen-King 392	

Do Not Cut on Diagonal Lines.

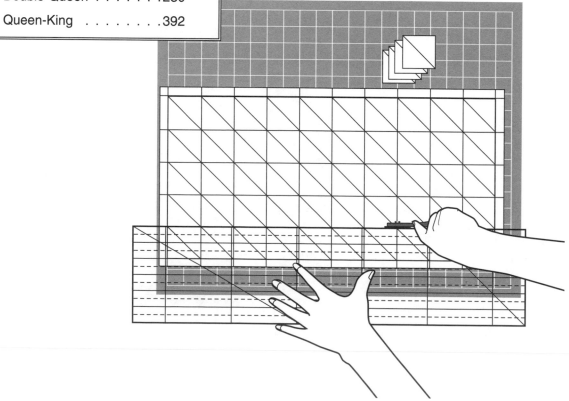

38

Sewing Star Points to Lattice

1. Stack all Lattice right side up.

2. Place the marked 2" squares wrong side up at your sewing machine.

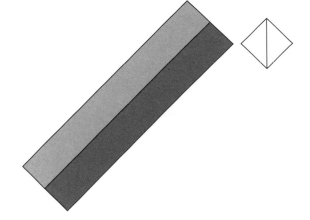

3. Place a 2" square right sides together to one Lattice, carefully lining up the outside edges, and overlapping the center seam.

   Check the diagonal line on each square. If the line is not drawn exactly corner to corner, replace it or redraw the line.

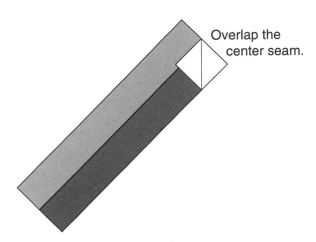

Overlap the center seam.

4. Place an "open toed" presser foot on your machine so you can see the needle sewing on the line.

5. Line up the needle with the diagonal line. Hold the threads, and sew on the diagonal line toward the outside edge. Carefully sew point to point.

6. Assembly-line sew a square to each pair, overlapping the top of the new Lattice each time. Do not clip the connecting threads.

   If lines are exceptionally dark on your light fabric, sew on the left edge of the line.

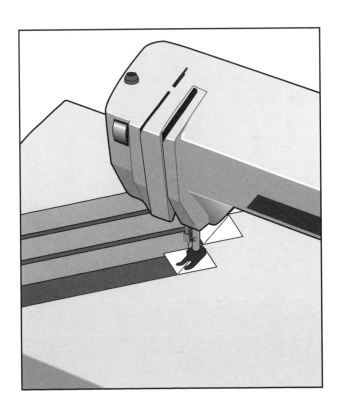

7. Turn the Lattice around, and assembly-line sew a second square to each pair. Clip connecting threads about every eighth Lattice to make chain manageable.

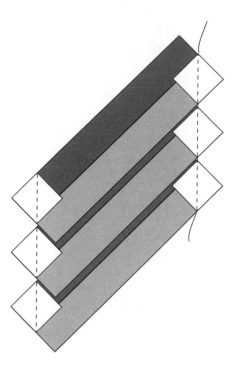

8. Trim seams to ¼" on both sides, rotary cutting with a 6" x 12" or 6" x 24" ruler as a guide, or free hand cut.

9. Clip the connecting threads.

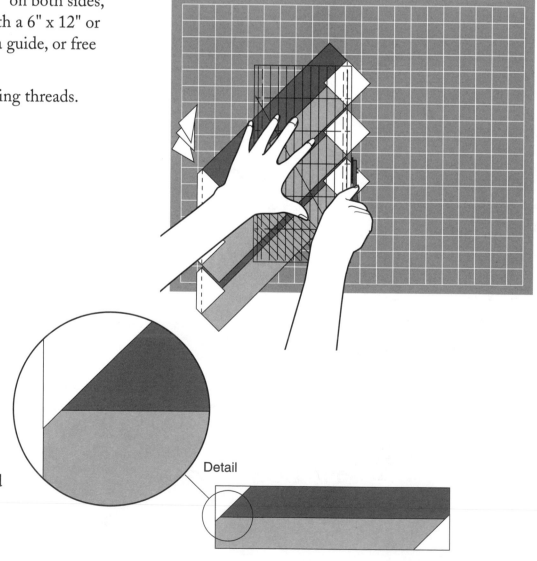

10. From the right side, set the seam, and press the triangles flat. Seams are pressed toward the Star Points.

Detail

11. Lay out Lattice in this order with 2" squares.

    Carefully match the outside edges.

    The 2" squares overlap each center seam and Star Point.

12. Carefully sew point to point. Assembly-line sew a third square to each pair.

    Do not clip the connecting threads.

13. Assembly-line sew a fourth square to each pair.

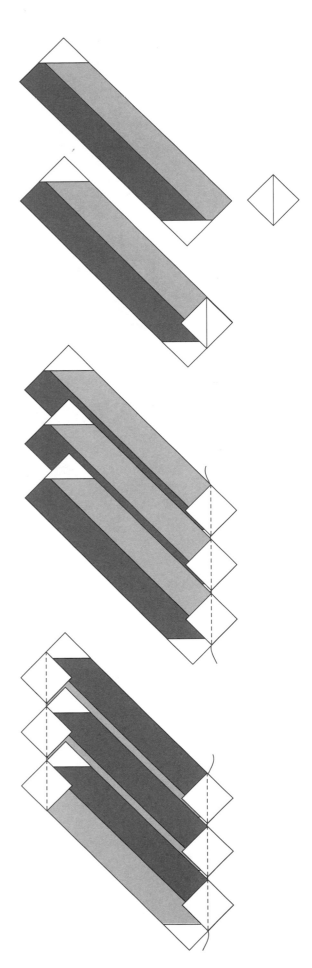

41

14. Trim seams to ¼" on both sides.
    Clip the connecting threads.

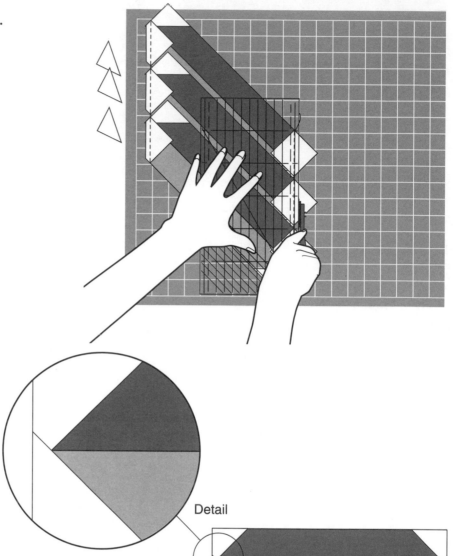

15. From the right side, press
    the triangles flat. Seams are
    pressed toward the
    Star Points.

16. Check for the ¼" seam
    allowance. The point should
    line up with the seam.

Detail

17. Square up uneven edges.

18. Set aside the remaining marked 2"
    squares for Star Points on the Frame
    and Border.

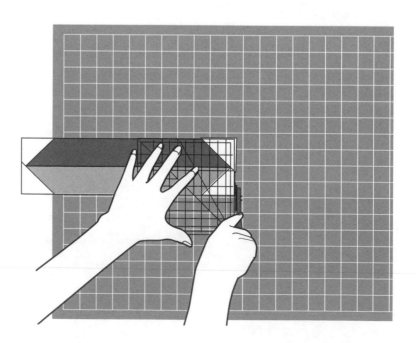

1. Lay out your blocks according to your choice.

2. Place Lattice with Star Points and Star Centers between blocks.

   Set aside remaining Star Centers for Frame.

3. Flip the second vertical row right sides together to the first vertical row.

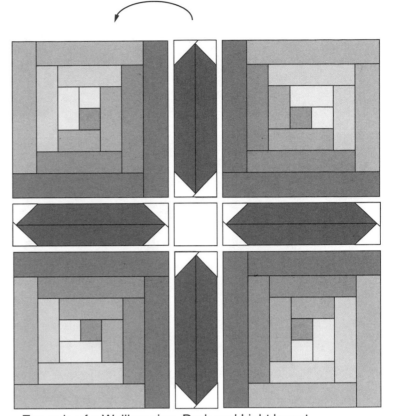

Example of a Wallhanging, Dark and Light layout.

4. Starting at the top of the row, stack up the pairs of pieces from the top to the bottom. The first pair will be at the top of your stack.

5. Lay the pile on your lap or to the left of your sewing machine.

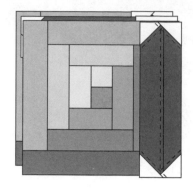

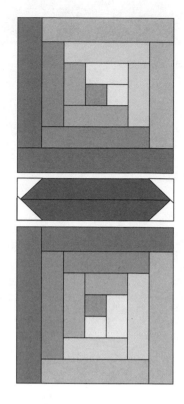

Use a ¼" seam allowance and 15 stitches per inch.

6. Pick up the first pair (Lattice and Block). Match the outside edges. Backstitch and sew.

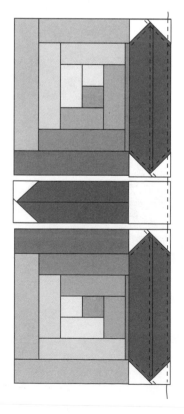

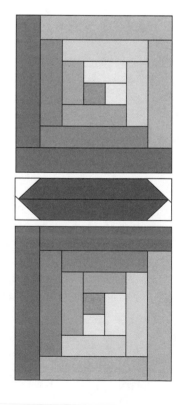

7. Pick up the next pair (Star Center Square and Lattice). Match the outside edges. Butt the pair against the first pair and sew.

   Open and check the Lattice to see if the stitching crosses the V of the Star for sharp points. If necessary, adjust your seam allowance.

8. Butt and sew the next pair.

9. Sew together all pairs in row, backstitching on bottom edge.

10. Open rows.

11. Do not clip threads joining the pieces.

Sewing the Third Vertical Row

1. Stack the third vertical row so the top Block is on the top of the stack. Place the stack to the right of your sewing machine.

2. Flip the Block to the Lattice in the second row. Match, backstitch, and stitch.

3. Flip the Lattice right side together to the Star Center Square in the second row. Match outside edges, butt, and sew.

4. Flip the Block to the Lattice of the second row. Ease or stretch the block to fit.

5. Assembly-line sew to the bottom of the third vertical row. Backstitch.

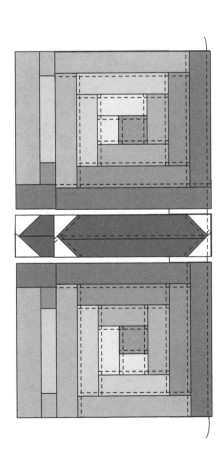

6. Stack and assembly-line sew all vertical rows. **Do not clip the threads joining the pieces.**

7. Lay out the quilt. Check to make sure every piece is in its proper position. It's much easier to rip out now if necessary.

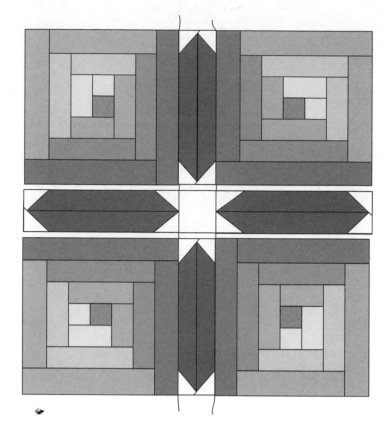

Sewing the Horizontal Rows

1. Flip the top row right sides together to the second row.

2. Match each piece, pushing the seams in opposite directions away from the Star Points.

3. Sew.

   Keep the row that you have just sewn on top so you can avoid twisting seams.

4. Continue until all horizontal rows are sewn.

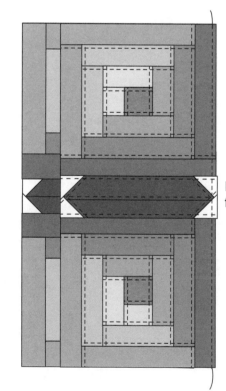

Push seams away from Star Points.

Pressing the Finished Top

1. From the wrong side, press seams away from Lattice. Press blocks flat as sewn.

2. Press from the right side.

1. Find and mark your layout choice with frame.

2. Note the fabrics and number needed for the Frame, made by sewing 2" x 42" strips together, pressing and cutting at your block size plus ⅛".

Fabric A ④   *Fabric B* ④
Frame ●   *Frame* ●

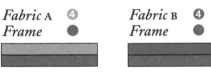

Sew at least 2 strips of each together. Cut them into 7 pieces.   *Sew at least 2 strips of each together. Cut them into 7 pieces.*

Example of a Lap Robe, Mountains layout.

47

3. Stack the 2" wide strips of A❹/Frame and B❹/Frame in equal piles according to your choice.

4. Assembly-line sew them together in pairs.

5. Set the seam. Lift strip and press seam allowance to one side.

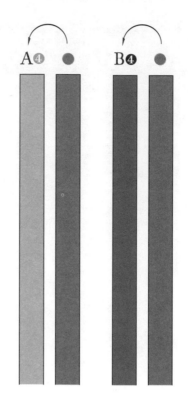

6. Transfer the size of the Block plus ⅛" from page 5. The Frame is cut this size.

Lattice and Frame Size

7. Cut the required number of Frame pieces from each pair of strips according to your pattern.

If you get only 3 pieces per strip, you need to sew more together to get the required number. The Yardage and Cutting Charts allowed for these extra strips.

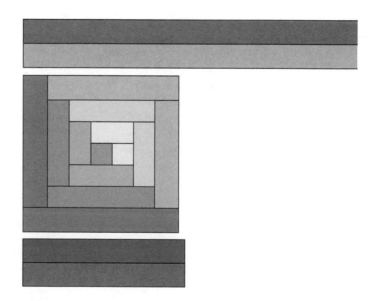

Sewing Star Points to the Frame

1. Stack all Frame pieces right side up. Place a marked 2" square wrong side up on the Frame.

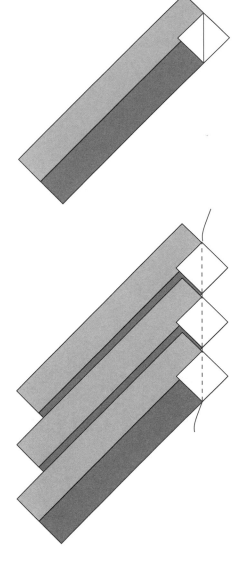

2. Assembly-line sew a square to each pair, overlapping the top of the new Frame each time.

3. Turn the pieces around, and assembly-line sew a second square to each pair. Clip into manageable "chains."

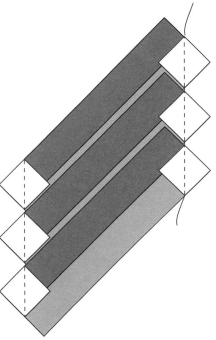

4. Trim seams to ¼" on both sides.

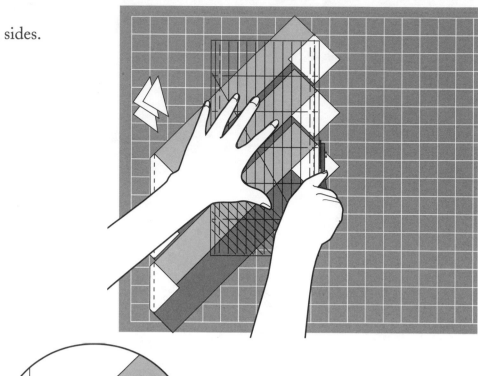

5. From the right side, press the triangles flat. The seam is pressed toward the Star Point.

Detail

6. Lay out the Frame pieces with 2" squares. Carefully match the outside edges.

7. Assembly-line sew a third and fourth square to each pair.

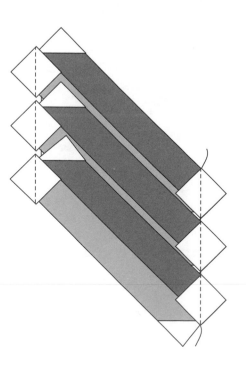

8. Trim seams to ¼" on both sides.

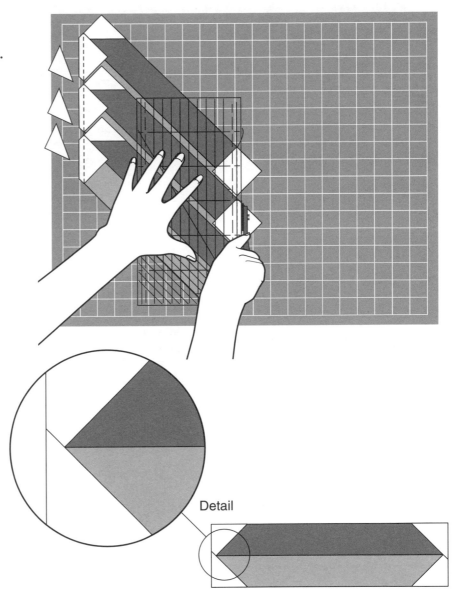

9. From the right side, press the triangles flat.

   Check for the ¼" seam allowance. The point should line up with the seam.

Detail

10. Square up the outside edges.

11. Set aside until First or Only Border pieces are completed.

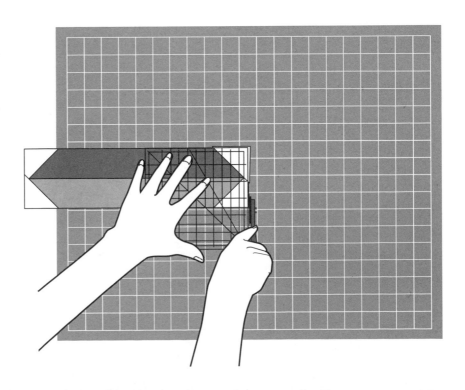

Making the First or Only Border

1. The First or Only Border is the same
width as the Lattice and Star Centers.
Transfer the measurement from page 5.

Record your
Width

approximately 3½"

2. Cut these Border strips selvage to selvage
at your measurement.

Cut this many strips
Wallhanging 4
Lap Robe 6
Twin 7
Double-Queen 8
Queen-King 10

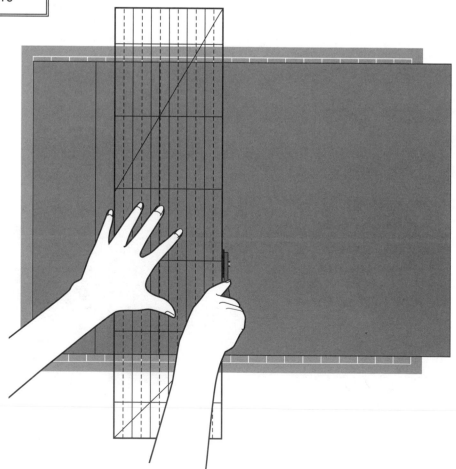

3. Layer cut the strips into the size of your
   block. Refer to page 5.

   Do not add on extra ⅛".

   Block Size [   ]

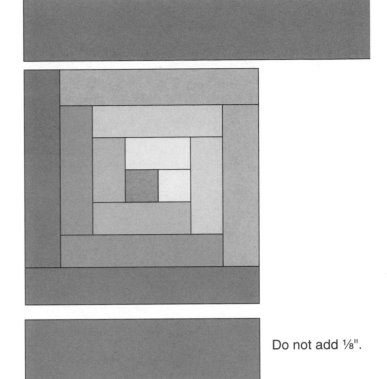

Cut this many block size pieces	
Wallhanging	8
Lap Robe	14
Twin	16
Double-Queen	20
Queen-King	24

Do not add ⅛".

4. From the remaining strips, layer cut Border
   Squares as needed, approximately 3½" square.

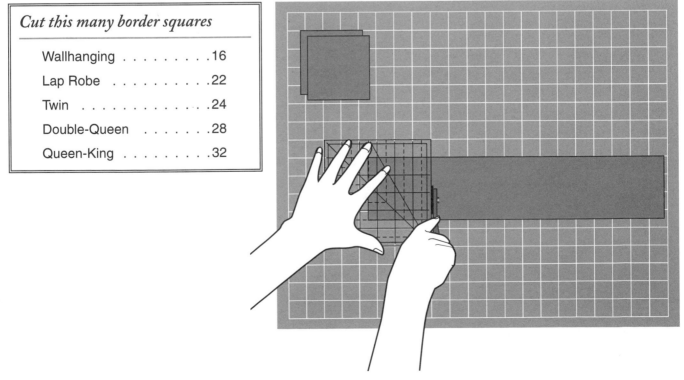

Cut this many border squares	
Wallhanging	16
Lap Robe	22
Twin	24
Double-Queen	28
Queen-King	32

Sewing Star Points to First Border Squares

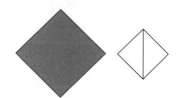

1. Count out four First Border Squares for corners. Set aside.

2. Stack all remaining First Border Squares right side up, and marked 2" Star Squares wrong side up.

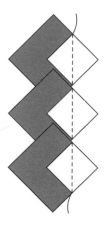

3. Place the Star Square on the Border Square. Carefully line up the outside edges.

4. Assembly-line sew, overlapping the top of the new square each time.

5. Trim seams to ¼".

6. Clip the connecting threads.

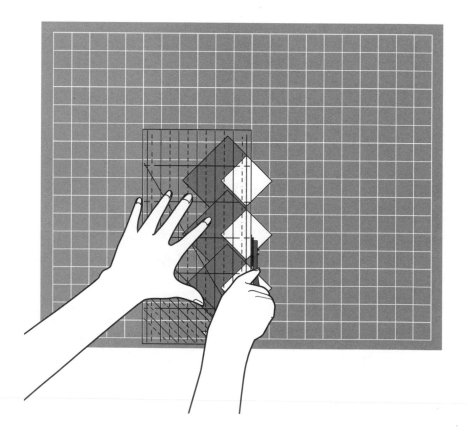

7. From the right side, press the triangles flat. Seams are pressed toward the Star Points.

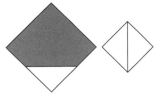

8. Place a second 2" Star Square on the Border Square. Carefully match the outside edges.

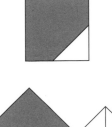

9. Assembly-line sew a second 2" Star Square to each Border Square. Do not clip the connecting threads.

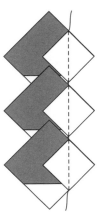

10. Trim seams to ¼". Clip the connecting threads.

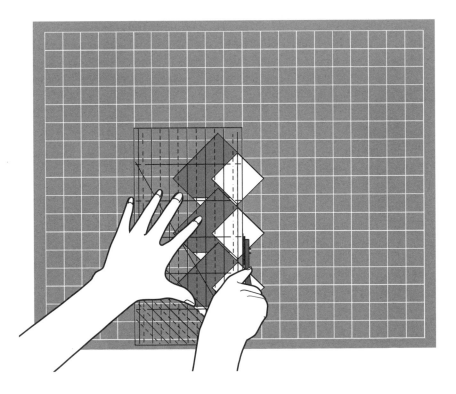

11. From the right side, press the triangles flat. Seams are pressed toward the Star Points.

12. Square up the outside edges. Check for the ¼" seam allowance.

Sewing the Frame and First or Only Border Together

1. Place Frame, Border, and Stars around the quilt top.

Example of a Wallhanging, Dark and Light layout.

2. On the left, flip the Frame row right sides together to the Border row. Repeat on the right side.

3. Starting at the top of the row, stack up the pairs of pieces from the top to the bottom. The first pair will be at the top of your stack.

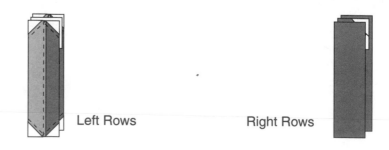

Left Rows   Right Rows

4. Assembly-line sew together all pairs in rows, backstitching on outside edges.

5. Open rows.

6. Flip the top row right sides together to the second row.

7. Match each piece, pushing the seams in opposite directions away from the Star Points.

8. Assembly-line sew.

   Keep the row that you have just sewn on top so you can avoid twisting seams.

9. Press the seams flat toward the Star Square and Border Square.

10. Pin and sew to sides of quilt top.

11. Press seams away from Frame.

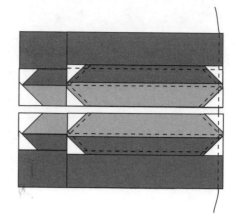

12. Sew Frame and Border to top and bottom, repeating same technique.

Pressing the Finished Top

1. From the wrong side press seams away from Frame. Press blocks flat as sewn.

2. Press from the right side.

58

Adding the Borders

Designing Your Borders

Be creative when adding borders. Suggested border yardage and border examples are given for each quilt. However, you may wish to custom design the borders by changing the widths of the strips. This might change backing and batting yardage.

When custom fitting the quilt, lay the top on your bed before adding the borders and backing. Measure to find how much border is needed to get the fit you want. Keep in mind that the quilt will "shrink" approximately 3" in the length and width after machine quilting.

Piecing Borders and Binding Strips

1. Stack and square off the ends of each strip, trimming away the selvage edges.

2. Seam the strips of each fabric into long pieces by assembly-line sewing. Lay the first strip right side up. Lay the second strip right sides to it. Backstitch, stitch the short ends together, and backstitch again.

3. Take the strip on the top and fold it so the right side is up.

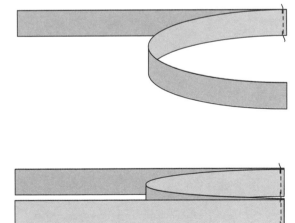

4. Place the third strip right sides to it, backstitch, stitch, and backstitch again.

5. Continue assembly-line sewing all the short ends together into long pieces for each fabric.

6. Clip the threads holding the strips together.

7. Press seams to one side.

Sewing the Borders to the Quilt Top

1. Measure down the center to find the length. Cut two side strips that measurement plus two inches.

2. Right sides together, match and pin the center of the strips to the center of the sides. Pin at ends, allowing an extra inch of border at each end. Pin intermittently.

3. Sew with the quilt on top. Set the seams and press toward the borders.

4. Square the ends even with the top and bottom of the quilt.

5. Measure the width across the center including newly added borders. Cut two strips that measurement plus two inches.

6. Right sides together, match and pin intermittently, allowing an extra inch of border at both ends. Sew with the quilt on top.

7. Set the seams and press toward the borders.

8. Square the ends even with the side borders.

   Repeat these steps for additional borders.

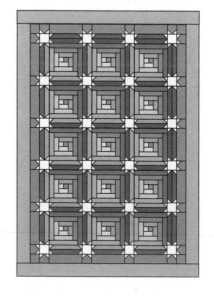

Machine Quilting

Layering Quilt Top with Backing and Batting

1. Piece the backing yardage together for larger size quilts.

   The seams may run down the center back or across the width, whichever works better for your yardage.

   If the backing is smaller than the quilt top, consider piecing extra fabric together to make it large enough. The backing can then look as creative as the front.

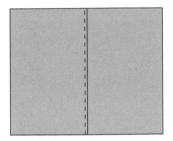

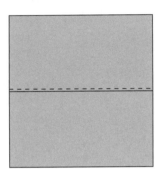

2. Stretch out the backing right side down on a large floor area or table. Tape down on a floor area or clamp onto a table with large binder clips.

3. Place and smooth out the thin batting on top.

4. Lay the quilt top right side up and centered on top of the batting.

5. Completely smooth all layers until they are flat.

6. Tape or clip securely. The backing and batting should extend at least 2" on all sides.

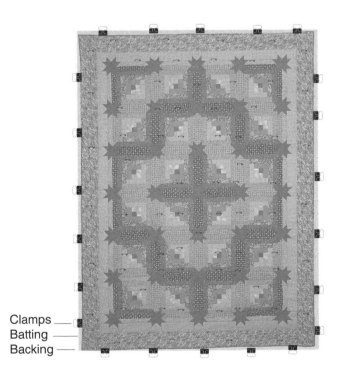

Clamps
Batting
Backing

Marking the Quilt Top

Decide where you want the quilting lines. Choose between straight diagonal lines and "stitching in the ditch," also called "stairstep quilting."

Straight

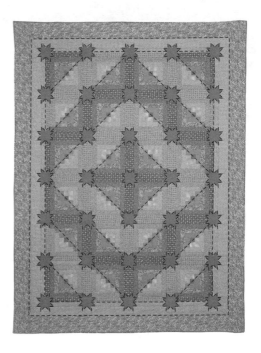

Marking straight diagonal lines across the center of each block, accenting the pattern, is the easiest.

1. With the 6" x 24" ruler, lightly mark the lines for machine quilting. *Make certain that you can remove the marks from the fabric.*

Suggested markers are...

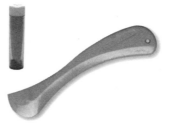

- Chaco™
- thin dry sliver of soap
- Hera™ marking tool
- Silver Pencil.

2. If you choose to outline the star, sew only one half of the star at a time.

3. Sew the second half of the star after the diagonal rows are stitched.

Stairstep

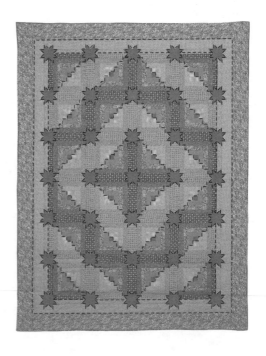

If you plan to "stitch in the ditch" around each star and "log", lines don't need to be marked. Follow the lines of the fabric. Sew only one half of the star at a time.

If you are experienced with "free motion machine quilting," it's easier to "stitch in the ditch" using your darning foot or spring needle with disengaged feed dogs.

Quick and Easy Safety Pin Basting

Place safety pins throughout the quilt away from the planned or marked quilting lines. Begin pinning in the center and work to the outside, spacing pins every 5".

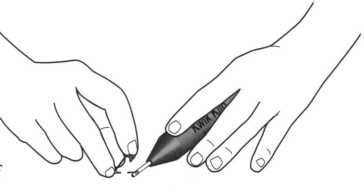

Grasp the opened pin in your right hand and the pinning tool in your left hand. Push the pin through the three layers, and bring the tip of the pin back out. Catch the tip in the groove of the tool and allow point to extend far enough to push pin closure down.

Machine Quilting the Marked Lines

Use a walking foot attachment for straight line quilting. Use invisible or regular matching thread in the top of your machine.

* invisible thread, loosen the top tension.

* regular thread, match the colors to A and B as you machine quilt.

* regular thread in the bobbin to match the backing.

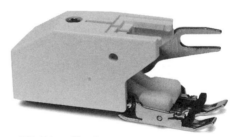

Walking Foot

Lengthen your stitch to 8 - 10 stitches per inch, or a #3 or #4 setting. Free arm machines need the "bed" placed for more surface area.

1. Trim the backing and batting to within 2" of the outside edge of the quilt.

2. Roll the quilt tightly from the outside edge in toward the middle. Hold this roll with quilt clips.

Jaws™

3. Slide this roll into the keyhole of the sewing machine. If necessary, rest the quilt roll on your left shoulder or lap.

4. Place the needle in the depth of the seam and pull up the bobbin thread. Lock the beginning and ending of each quilting line by backstitching. If available, use the "needle down" feature on your sewing machine.

5. Place your hands flat on both sides of the needle. Keep the quilt area flat and tight. If you need to ease in the top fabric, feed the quilt through the machine by pushing the layers of fabric and batting forward underneath the walking foot.

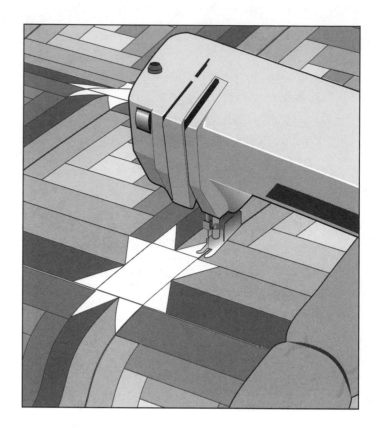

6. If puckering occurs on the backside, remove stitching by grasping the bobbin thread with a pin or tweezers and pull gently to expose the top thread. Touch the thread stitches with the rotary cutter blade as you pull the bobbin thread free from the quilt.

7. Unroll, roll, and machine quilt on all lines, sewing the length or width or diagonal of the quilt.

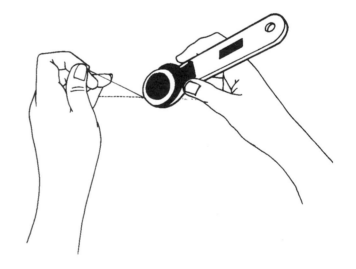

Adding the Binding

Use a walking foot attachment and regular thread on top and in the bobbin to match the binding. Use 10 stitches per inch, or #3 setting.

See page 59 to make one long binding strip.

1. Press the binding strip in half lengthwise with right sides out.

2. Line up the raw edges of the folded binding with the raw edge of the quilt top at the middle of one side.

3. Begin sewing 4" from the end of the binding.

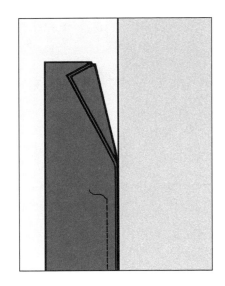

4. At the corner, stop the stitching ¼" from the edge with the needle in the fabric. Raise the presser foot and turn the quilt to the next side. Put the foot back down.

5. Sew backwards ¼" to the edge of the binding, raise the foot, and pull the quilt forward slightly.

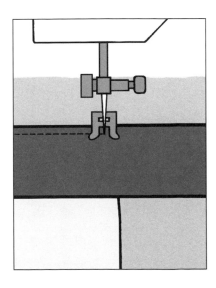

6. Fold the binding strip straight up on the diagonal. Fingerpress in the diagonal fold.

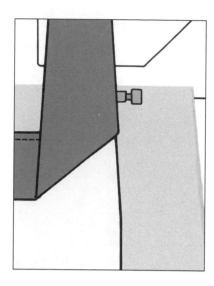

7. Fold the binding strip straight down with the diagonal fold underneath. Line up the top of the fold with the raw edge of the binding underneath.

8. Begin sewing from the corner.

9. Continue sewing and mitering the corners around the outside of the quilt.

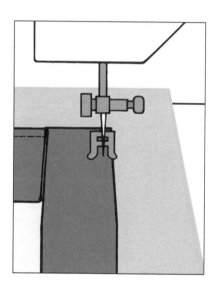

10. Stop sewing 4" from where the ends will overlap.

11. Line up the two ends of binding. Trim the excess with a ½" overlap.

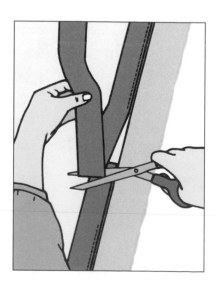

12. Open out the folded ends and pin right sides together. Sew a ¼" seam.

13. Continue to sew the binding in place.

14. Trim the batting and backing up to the raw edges of the binding.

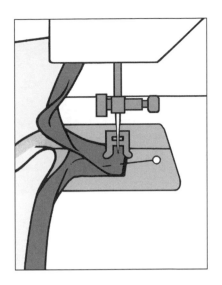

15. Fold the binding to the backside of the quilt. Pin in place so that the folded edge on the binding covers the stitching line. Tuck in the excess fabric at each miter on the diagonal.

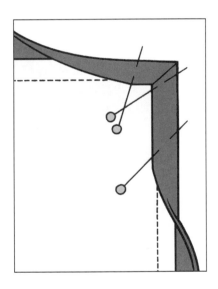

16. From the right side, "stitch in the ditch" using invisible or matching thread on the right side, and a bobbin thread to match the binding on the back side. Catch the folded edge of the binding on the back side with the stitching.

17. Sew an identification label on the backing.

Optional: Slipstitch the binding in place by hand.

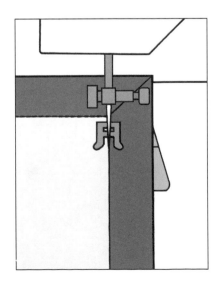

WALLHANGING LATTICE

Fabric A ❹
Fabric B ❹

*Sew at least 1 strip
of each together.
Cut it into 4 pieces.*

ALL SEVENS

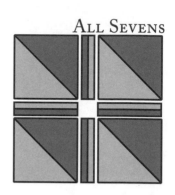

Fabric A ❹
Fabric A ❹

*Sew at least 1 strip
of each together.
Cut it into 2 pieces.*

Fabric B ❹
Fabric B ❹

*Sew at least 1 strip
of each together.
Cut it into 2 pieces.*

FIELDS & FURROWS

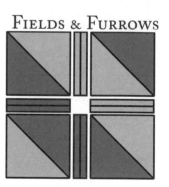

Fabric A ❹
Fabric A ❹

*Sew at least 1 strip
of each together.
Cut it into 4 pieces.*

LIGHT & DARK

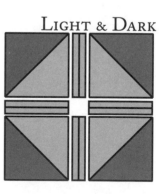

Fabric B ❹
Fabric B ❹

*Sew at least 1 strip
of each together.
Cut it into 4 pieces.*

DARK & LIGHT

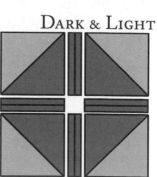

All Sevens

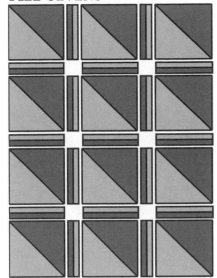

Fabric A ❹
Fabric B ❹

Sew at least 5 strips of each together. Cut them into 17 pieces.

Fields & Furrows

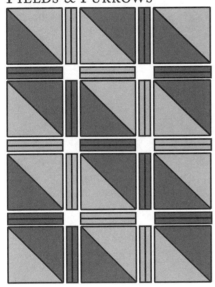

Fabric A ❹
Fabric A ❹

Sew at least 2 strips of each together. Cut them into 8 pieces.

Fabric B ❹
Fabric B ❹

Sew at least 3 strips of each together. Cut them into 9 pieces.

Mountains

Fabric A ❹
Fabric A ❹

Sew at least 1 strip of each together. Cut them into 4 pieces.

Fabric B ❹
Fabric B ❹

Sew at least 1 strip of each together. Cut them into 4 pieces.

Fabric A ❹
Fabric B ❹

Sew at least 3 strips of each together. Cut them into 9 pieces.

TWIN LATTICE

ALL SEVENS

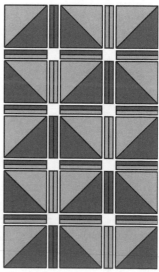

Fabric A ❹
Fabric B ❹

Sew at least 6 strips
of each together.
Cut them into 22
pieces.

FIELDS & FURROWS

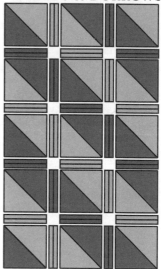

Fabric A ❹
Fabric A ❹

Sew at least 3 strips
of each together.
Cut them into 11
pieces.

Fabric B ❹
Fabric B ❹

Sew at least 3 strips
of each together.
Cut them into 11
pieces.

MOUNTAINS

Fabric A ❹
Fabric A ❹

Sew at least 2 strips
of each together.
Cut them into 5
pieces.

Fabric B ❹
Fabric B ❹

Sew at least 2 strips
of each together.
Cut them into 5
pieces.

Fabric A ❹
Fabric B ❹

Sew at least 3 strips
of each together.
Cut them into 12
pieces.

ALL SEVENS

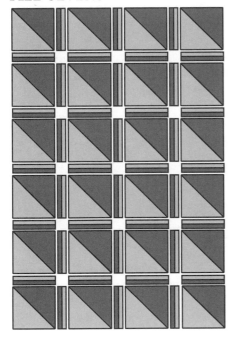

Fabric A ❹
Fabric B ❹

Sew at least 10 strips of each together. Cut them into 38 pieces.

FIELDS & FURROWS

Fabric A ❹
Fabric A ❹

Sew at least 5 strips of each together. Cut them into 19 pieces.

Fabric B ❹
Fabric B ❹

Sew at least 5 strips of each together. Cut them into 19 pieces.

LIGHT & DARK

Fabric A ❹
Fabric A ❹

Sew at least 6 strips
of each together.
Cut them into 24
pieces.

Fabric B ❹
Fabric B ❹

Sew at least 4 strips
of each together.
Cut them into 14
pieces.

DARK & LIGHT

Fabric A ❹
Fabric A ❹

Sew at least 4 strips
of each together.
Cut them into 14
pieces.

Fabric B ❹
Fabric B ❹

Sew at least 6 strips
of each together.
Cut them into 24
pieces.

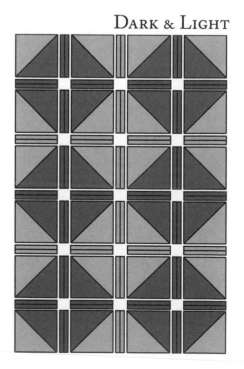

ZIG - ZAG

Fabric A ④
Fabric A ④

Fabric B ④
Fabric B ④

Sew at least 5 strips of each together. Cut them into 17 pieces.

Sew at least 6 strips of each together. Cut them into 21 pieces.

MOUNTAINS

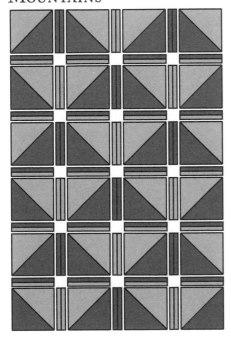

Fabric A ④
Fabric A ④

Fabric B ④
Fabric B ④

Fabric A ④
Fabric B ④

Sew at least 3 strips of each together. Cut them into 9 pieces.

Sew at least 3 strips of each together. Cut them into 9 pieces.

Sew at least 5 strips of each together. Cut them into 20 pieces.

MIRROR IMAGE

Fabric A ④
Fabric A ④

Sew at least 3 strips
of each together.
Cut them into 12
pieces.

Fabric B ❹
Fabric B ❹

Sew at least 3 strips
of each together.
Cut them into 12
pieces.

Fabric A ④
Fabric B ❹

Sew at least 4 strips
of each together.
Cut them into 14
pieces.

BARN RAISING

Fabric A ④
Fabric A ④

Sew at least 5 strips
of each together.
Cut them into 20
pieces.

Fabric B ❹
Fabric B ❹

Sew at least 5 strips
of each together.
Cut them into 18
pieces.

ALL SEVENS

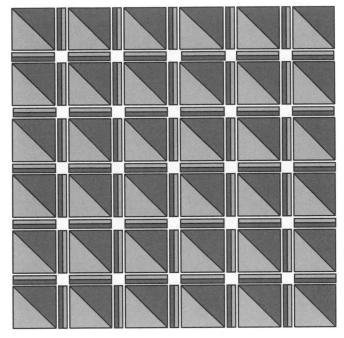

PRAIRIE PIONEER QUILTERS
of GRAND ISLAND, NEBRASKA

Fabric A ❹
Fabric B ❹

Sew at least 15 strips
of each together.
Cut them into 60
pieces.

FIELDS & FURROWS

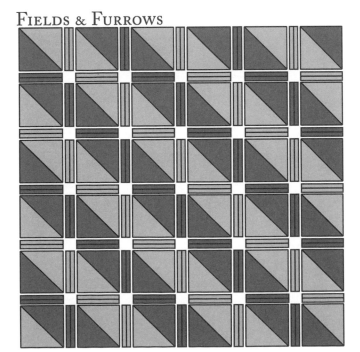

Fabric A ❹   *Fabric* B ❹
Fabric A ❹   *Fabric* B ❹

Sew at least 8 strips   Sew at least 8 strips
of each together.   of each together.
Cut them into 30   Cut them into 30
pieces.   pieces.

LIGHT & DARK

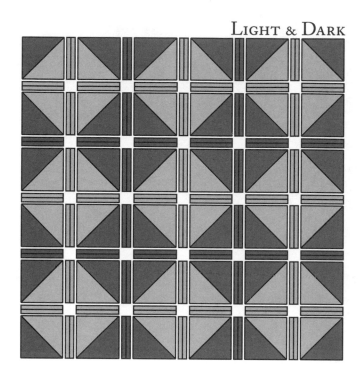

Fabric A ④
Fabric A ④

Fabric B ④
Fabric B ④

Sew at least 9 strips
of each together.
Cut them into 36
pieces.

Sew at least 6 strips
of each together.
Cut them into 24
pieces.

DARK & LIGHT

Fabric A ④
Fabric A ④

Fabric B ④
Fabric B ④

Sew at least 6 strips
of each together.
Cut them into 24
pieces.

Sew at least 9 strips
of each together.
Cut them into 36
pieces.

ZIG - ZAG

Fabric A ④
Fabric A ④

Sew at least 7 strips of each together. Cut them into 27 pieces.

Fabric B ④
Fabric B ④

Sew at least 9 strips of each together. Cut them into 33 pieces.

MOUNTAINS

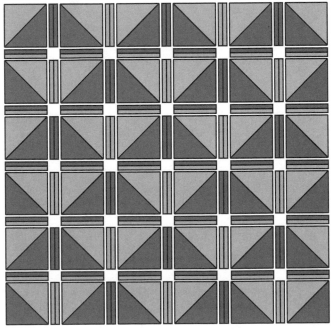

Fabric A ④
Fabric A ④

Sew at least 4 strips of each together. Cut them into 15 pieces.

Fabric B ④
Fabric B ④

Sew at least 4 strips of each together. Cut them into 15 pieces.

Fabric A ④
Fabric B ④

Sew at least 8 strips of each together. Cut them into 30 pieces.

Star

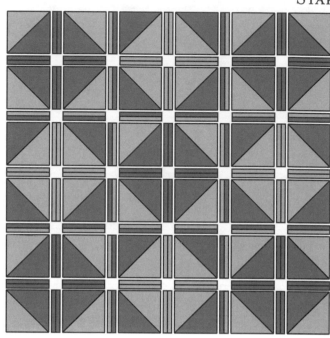

Fabric A ❹
Fabric A ❹

Sew at least 4 strips of each together. Cut them into 16 pieces.

Fabric B ❹
Fabric B ❹

Sew at least 5 strips of each together. Cut them into 20 pieces.

Fabric A ❹
Fabric B ❹

Sew at least 6 strips of each together. Cut them into 24 pieces.

Barn Raising

Fabric A ❹
Fabric A ❹

Sew at least 7 strips of each together. Cut them into 28 pieces.

Fabric B ❹
Fabric B ❹

Sew at least 8 strips of each together. Cut them into 32 pieces.

WALLHANGING FRAME

ALL SEVENS

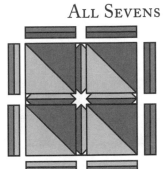

Fabric A
Frame ●

Sew at least 1 strip
of each together.
Cut it into 4 pieces.

Fabric B ❹
Frame ●

Sew at least 1 strip
of each together.
Cut it into 4 pieces.

FIELDS & FURROWS

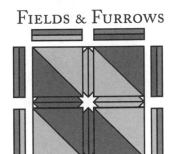

Fabric A ❹
Frame ●

Sew at least 1 strip
of each together.
Cut it into 4 pieces.

Fabric B ❹
Frame ●

Sew at least 1 strip
of each together.
Cut it into 4 pieces.

LIGHT & DARK

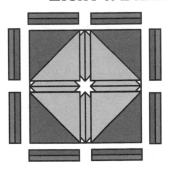

Fabric B ❹
Frame ●

Sew at least 2 strips
of each together.
Cut them into 8
pieces.

DARK & LIGHT

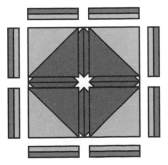

Fabric A
Frame ●

Sew at least 2 strips
of each together.
Cut them into 8
pieces.

All Sevens

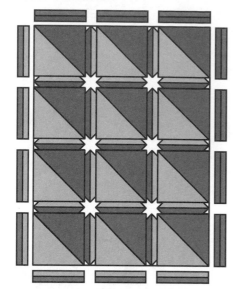

Fabric A
Frame ●

Sew at least 2 strips of each together. Cut them into 7 pieces.

Fabric B
Frame ●

Sew at least 2 strips of each together. Cut them into 7 pieces.

Fields & Furrows

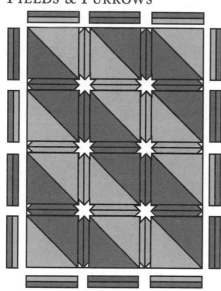

Fabric A ④
Frame ●

Sew at least 2 strips of each together. Cut them into 8 pieces.

Fabric B ④
Frame ●

Sew at least 2 strips of each together. Cut them into 6 pieces.

Mountains

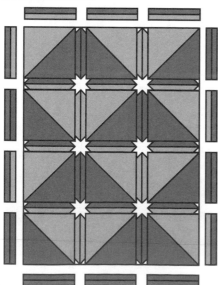

Fabric A ④
Frame ●

Sew at least 2 strips of each together. Cut them into 7 pieces.

Fabric B
Frame ●

Sew at least 2 strips of each together. Cut them into 7 pieces.

TWIN FRAME

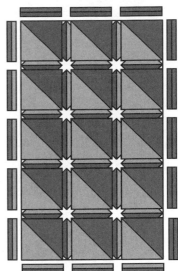

Fabric A ④
Frame ●

Fabric B ④
Frame ●

Sew at least 2 strips of each together. Cut them into 8 pieces.

Sew at least 2 strips of each together. Cut them into 8 pieces.

FIELDS & FURROWS

Fabric A ④
Frame ●

Fabric B ④
Frame ●

Sew at least 2 strips of each together. Cut them into 8 pieces.

Sew at least 2 strips of each together. Cut them into 8 pieces.

MOUNTAINS

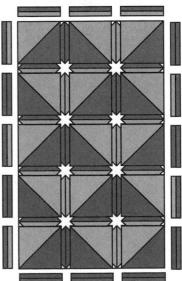

Fabric A ④
Frame ●

Fabric B ④
Frame ●

Sew at least 2 strips of each together. Cut them into 8 pieces.

Sew at least 2 strips of each together. Cut them into 8 pieces.

ALL SEVENS

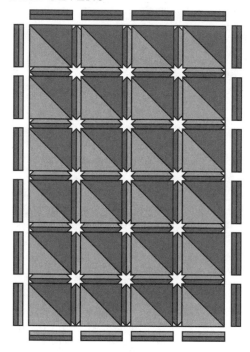

Fabric A ❹
Frame ●

Fabric B ❹
Frame ●

Sew at least 3 strips of each together. Cut them into 10 pieces.

Sew at least 3 strips of each together. Cut them into 10 pieces.

FIELDS & FURROWS

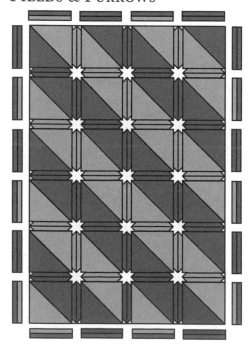

Fabric A ❹
Frame ●

Fabric B ❹
Frame ●

Sew at least 3 strips of each together. Cut them into 10 pieces.

Sew at least 3 strips of each together. Cut them into 10 pieces.

DOUBLE-QUEEN FRAME

LIGHT & DARK

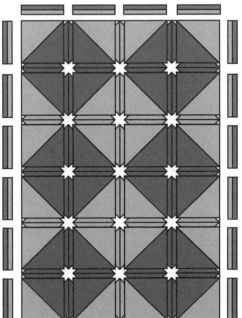

Fabric B ❹
Frame ●

Sew at least 5 strips
of each together.
Cut them into 20
pieces.

DARK & LIGHT

Fabric A ❹
Frame ●

Sew at least 5 strips
of each together.
Cut them into 20
pieces.

ZIG - ZAG

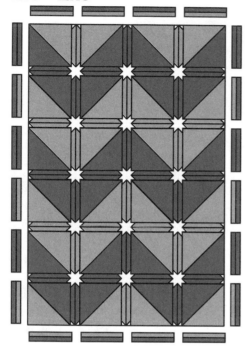

Fabric A ④
Frame ⬤

Sew at least 4 strips of each together. Cut them into 14 pieces.

Fabric B ④
Frame ⬤

Sew at least 2 strips of each together. Cut them into 6 pieces.

MOUNTAINS

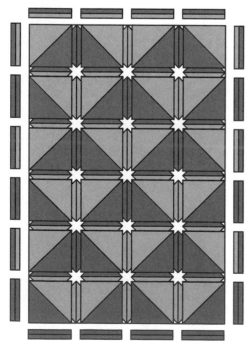

Fabric A ④
Frame ⬤

Sew at least 3 strips of each together. Cut them into 10 pieces.

Fabric B ④
Frame ⬤

Sew at least 3 strips of each together. Cut them into 10 pieces.

DOUBLE-QUEEN FRAME

Fabric A ❹
Frame ●

Fabric B ❹
Frame ●

Sew at least 3 strips of each together. Cut them into 10 pieces.

Sew at least 3 strips of each together. Cut them into 10 pieces.

BARN RAISING

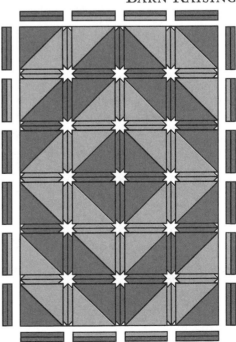

Fabric A ❹
Frame ●

Fabric B ❹
Frame ●

Sew at least 2 strips of each together. Cut them into 8 pieces.

Sew at least 3 strips of each together. Cut them into 12 pieces.

ALL SEVENS

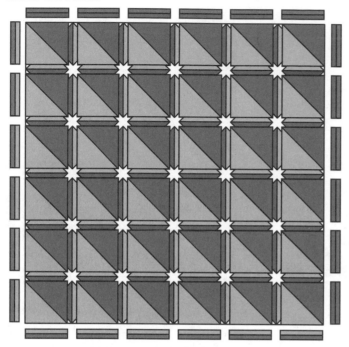

Fabric A ❹
Frame ●

Sew at least 4 strips of each together. Cut them into 12 pieces.

Fabric B ❹
Frame ●

Sew at least 3 strips of each together. Cut them into 12 pieces.

FIELDS & FURROWS

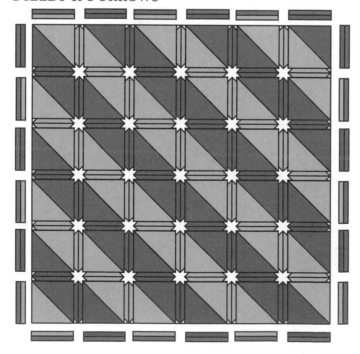

Fabric A ❹
Frame ●

Sew at least 3 strips of each together. Cut them into 12 pieces.

Fabric B ❹
Frame ●

Sew at least 3 strips of each together. Cut them into 12 pieces.

QUEEN–KING FRAME

LIGHT & DARK

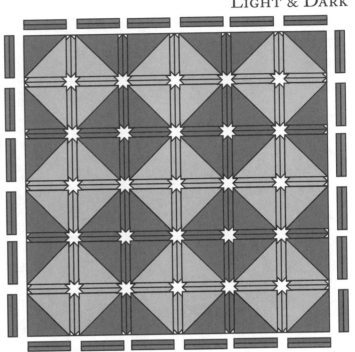

Fabric B ❹
Frame ●

Sew at least 6 strips of each together. Cut them into 24 pieces.

DARK & LIGHT

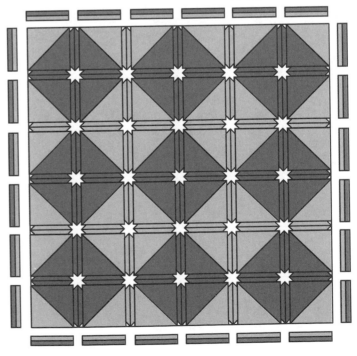

Fabric A ❹
Frame ●

Sew at least 6 strips of each together. Cut them into 24 pieces.

ZIG - ZAG

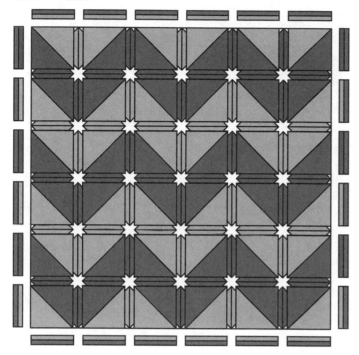

Fabric A ④
Frame ●

Sew at least 5 strips of each together. Cut them into 18 pieces.

Fabric B ④
Frame ●

Sew at least 2 strips of each together. Cut them into 6 pieces.

MOUNTAINS

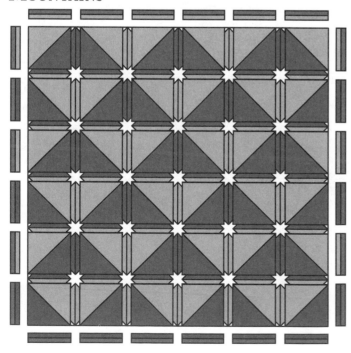

Fabric A ④
Frame ●

Sew at least 3 strips of each together. Cut them into 12 pieces.

Fabric B ④
Frame ●

Sew at least 3 strips of each together. Cut them into 12 pieces.

STAR

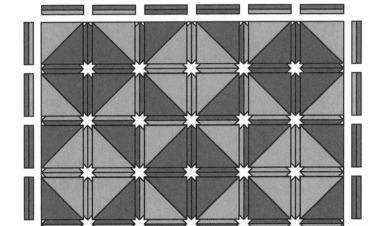

Fabric A ❹
Frame ●

Fabric B ❹
Frame ●

Sew at least 4 strips of each together. Cut them into 16 pieces.

Sew at least 2 strips of each together. Cut them into 8 pieces.

BARN RAISING

Fabric A ❹
Frame ●

Fabric B ❹
Frame ●

Sew at least 4 strips of each together. Cut them into 16 pieces.

Sew at least 2 strips of each together. Cut them into 8 pieces.

INDEX

ORDER INFORMATION

Quilt in a Day books offer a wide range of techniques and are directed toward a variety of skill levels. If you do not have a quilt shop in your area, you may write for a complete catalog and current price list of all books and patterns published by Quilt in a Day®, Inc., 1955 Diamond Street, San Marcos, CA 92069 or call 1-760-591-0082 or order toll free 1(800)777-4852

Easy

These books are easy enough for beginners of any age.
Log Cabin Quilt in a Day
Irish Chain
Bits & Pieces
Trip Around the World
Heart's Delight
Scrap Quilt
Rail Fence
Flying Geese
Star for all Seasons
Winning Hand
Courthouse Steps

Applique

While these books offer a variety of techniques, easy applique is featured in each.

Applique in a Day
Dresden Plate
Sunbonnet Sue Visits Quilt in a Day
Recycled Treasures
Creating with Color
Spools & Tools

Intermediate to Advanced

With a little Quilt in a Day experience, these books offer a rewarding project.
Trio of Treasured Quilts
Lover's Knot
Amish Quilt
May Basket
Morning Star
Friendship Quilt
Tulip Quilt
Burgoyne Surrounded
Snowball
Tulip Table Runner

Holiday

When a favorite holiday is approaching, Quilt in a Day is there to help you plan.
Country Christmas
Bunnies & Blossoms
Patchwork Santa
Last Minute Gifts
Angel of Antiquity
Log Cabin Wreath
Log Cabin Tree
Country Flag
Lover's Knot Placemats

Sampler

Always and forever popular are books with a variety of patterns.
The Sampler
Block Party Series 1, Quilter's Year
Block Party Series 2, Baskets and Flowers
Block Party Series 3, Quilters' Almanac
Block Party Series 4, Christmas Traditions
Block Party Series 5, Pioneer Sampler

Angle Piecing

Quilt in a Day "template free" methods make angle cutting less of a challenge.
Diamond Log Cabin
Pineapple Quilt
Blazing Star Tablecloth
Schoolhouse
Radiant Star
Star Log Cabin

THANKS ...

Special thanks to these Star Studded Quiltmakers:

Sue Bouchard

Carol Neumann

Barbara Spencer

Maryalice Baldwin

Sincere gratitude to Marilyn and Vern Dorn for the use of their beautiful log home, located in Big Bear, California.